Grade 5

Scott Foresman

Fresh Reads
for Fluency and Comprehension

Glenview, Illinois • Boston, Massachusetts • Chandler, Arizona • Upper Saddle River, New Jersey

ISBN 13: 978-0-328-48897-1
ISBN 10:   0-328-48897-6
9 10 V0N4 18 17 16 15 14 13

Contents

Unit 1 Meeting Challenges

Unit 2 Doing the Right Thing

Unit 3 Inventors and Artists

Unit 4 Adapting

Unit 5 Adventurers

Unit 6 The Unexpected

Fresh Reads

Name _____

Read the selection. Then answer the questions that follow.

The Dog and the Cows

One day a smart but tired dog came to a green pasture where three cows were grazing. He thought the quiet happy cows would be good company.

However, the cows came over and formed a half-circle so that he could not go forward or go left or right to enter the pasture.

"Why should we share our pasture with you?" one said sternly.

"Because I'm tired of being alone, and I don't eat grass," the dog said.

The cows murmured to each other. "All right, you may stay," they said.

When the farmer arrived, the dog remembered his old job. Suddenly he barked and ran and nipped at the cows' ankles to herd them over to the farmer. The farmer laughed and patted the dog's head. He took the dog home, but the dog had to sleep in the barn with the cows, who took some time to forgive him.

Turn the page.

Answer the questions below.

1 Why did the cows form a half-circle?

  A They were grazing in the same small area.

  B They were blocking the dog's way.

  C The best grass grew in that corner of the pasture.

  D The farmer had called them over.

2 What is the climax of this story?

  F The farmer arrives.

  G The dog herds the cows.

  H The farmer takes the dog home.

  J The cows forgive the dog.

3 Which of the following events happened *first*?

  A The cows formed a half-circle.

  B The farmer took the dog home.

  C The dog learned to herd cows.

  D The cows murmured to the dog.

4 What is the dog's reason for herding the cows?

_____

_____

_____

_____

_____

_____

_____

_____

_____

Name _____

Read the selection. Then answer the questions that follow.

The Fox and the Rooster

One morning, a hungry fox trotted along looking for his breakfast. As he passed a farm, he heard a rooster crow. The fox licked his chops and looked around, hoping to sight the rooster. Finally he spied the bird sitting high in a tree.

"Good morning, friend!" the fox called out. "Come down and have a friendly chat with me!"

"Oh, I can't do that," replied the rooster. "You would eat me for sure."

"You haven't heard the news, then," the fox said in a surprised tone. "All of us animals have agreed to live peacefully from now on. We aren't allowed to eat one another anymore."

The rooster did not answer. Instead, he began to look into the distance with great interest. He cocked his head as if he heard something, but the fox heard nothing. As a result, the fox became curious.

"What's going on?" asked the fox. "What do you see? What do you hear?"

"Why, it's a pack of wolves running this way. They must be coming for a friendly visit, just as you did," said the rooster.

"Oh!" said the fox nervously. "Now that I've told you the news, I'll just move along."

"Why not stay and visit with all of us," asked the rooster, "if what you say is true and all the animals are living in peace?"

"The word may not have gotten around to the wolves!" the fox said as he hurried away.

Turn the page.

Answer the questions below.

1 **Why did the fox become curious?**

 A He heard the wolves.

 B He was looking for something to eat.

 C The rooster looked into the distance.

 D The rooster was in a tree.

2 **What was the main conflict in the story?**

 F The fox wanted to eat the rooster.

 G The rooster wanted to escape the wolves.

 H The wolves wanted to eat the fox.

 J The rooster wanted the fox to stay.

3 **The rooster thought the fox was**

 A smart.

 B friendly.

 C angry.

 D dishonest.

4 **In this story, when does the rooster *first* begin to fool the fox?**

 F when the rooster sits by himself high in the tree

 G when the rooster tips his head as if to hear better

 H when the rooster says that the wolves are coming

 J when the rooster invites the fox to stay and visit

5 **Do you think wolves were really coming toward the rooster and the fox? Explain your answer.**

_____

_____

_____

_____

_____

_____

Name _____

Read the selection. Then answer the questions that follow.

The Old Gentleman and the Doctor

Once there was an old gentleman who suddenly lost his sight. He lived in a very large house on a hill. By moving from tree to tree, he made his way carefully down and into town. He asked the first person he met to lead him to Dr. Brown's office. Dr. Brown was not a very good physician. He loved to read and was distracted by books. He talked often about novels instead of a patient's problem. He was, however, the only town doctor.

"If you restore my sight," the old gentleman said, "I will be able to read again and I will talk to you about books. If you talk about books instead of helping me, I will remain blind, and you will have no one to really listen to you."

The doctor was surprised. In truth, he did not realize how much his talk of books got in the way of helping people. Nor did he realize how lonely he was for someone to really listen to him. And so he turned from novels to medical books and found a way to cure the old gentleman. While gathering this medical information, the doctor kept seeing his other patients. He was astonished by how much happier they seemed when he had no new books to talk about. It occurred to him that they needed someone to listen to them too. And so everything changed. The old gentleman's sight was restored, and the two readers exchanged books and sometimes talked late into the evening. You might say that the old gentleman cured the doctor's blindness too.

Turn the page.

Answer the questions below.

1 **Why did the old gentleman choose Dr. Brown?**

A He thought he could help Dr. Brown.

B He knew Dr. Brown liked books.

C Dr. Brown's office was closest.

D There were no other doctors in town.

2 **When did the doctor learn how much listening to his patients mattered to them?**

F before the old gentleman came to the office

G after discussing the treatment with the old gentleman

H before exchanging any books with the old gentleman

J after the old gentleman listened to his advice

3 **Which word best describes the old gentleman?**

A trusting

B proud

C fearful

D fair

4 **In what way is the doctor "blind" in the first part of the story?**

_____

_____

_____

_____

5 **How did the change in Dr. Brown's treatment of his patients make them happier?**

_____

_____

_____

_____

_____

Name _____

Read the selection. Then answer the questions that follow.

Why the Raven Is Black

The people of the far north tell this story about Owl and Raven, who were best friends. One day, Raven made a lovely new dress for Owl. Since Raven had been so nice, Owl then began to make a white dress for Raven. Owl worked at night by the light of a lamp that burned heavy oil. Owl tried to measure Raven for the dress, but Raven kept hopping around.

"Oh, I'm going to be so beautiful!" Raven cried as she hopped.

"Stop that hopping," Owl warned. "You'll knock over the lamp."

But Raven would not stand still. Just as owl had predicted, Raven finally knocked over the lamp. The black oil spilled all over the white dress. That is why Raven is black.

Turn the page.

Answer the questions below.

1 Why did Owl begin to make a dress for Raven?

A because Raven had made a dress for Owl

B because Raven would not stand still

C because Raven's dress had been ruined

D because Raven did not like Owl's dress

2 What happened when Raven knocked over the lamp?

F Owl told Raven to stop hopping.

G Raven was excited about the new dress.

H Owl's dress was ruined.

J Black oil spilled on Raven's dress.

3 Which of the following words best describes Raven's actions?

A wise

B careless

C lazy

D honest

4 What color would Raven be if she had not knocked over the lamp? Explain your answer.

_____

_____

_____

_____

_____

_____

_____

_____

_____

_____

Name _____

Read the selection. Then answer the questions that follow.

The Cricket and the Mountain Lion

The Native Americans of California tell this story about a cricket who chased away a mountain lion. The mountain lion jumped onto a hollow log and sat down. Before he had settled down, a cricket hopped out of the log and scolded him.

"Get off my roof, trespasser!" Cricket yelled.

Lion just looked at Cricket. He could not believe that this tiny creature was telling him what to do. He climbed off the log and crouched low on the ground, eye to eye with Cricket.

"I am the chief of the whole animal tribe," said Lion haughtily. "I can do as I please. Why, I could crush your house with one paw!"

"If you did, you'd be sorry," said Cricket. "My cousin will come after you if you do anything like that."

"I am not afraid of any insect," Lion growled. "Tell your cousin to meet us here tomorrow. If he can make me run away, I will never bother you again. If he can't, well, you better get ready to move."

The next morning, Lion returned to Cricket's log. As he called out to Cricket, he heard a buzzing in his ear. Suddenly that ear began to sting and itch, and Lion howled in pain.

"Meet my cousin, Mosquito," said Cricket.

Lion scratched his ear furiously, shook his head, and begged Cricket to make Mosquito leave him alone.

"That's enough, Cousin," said Cricket. Mosquito flew out of Lion's ear. Lion bounded away as fast as he could. And he never came back.

Turn the page.

Answer the questions below.

1 Why did Cricket scream at Lion?

A Lion threatened Cricket.

B Lion crushed Cricket's house.

C Lion sat on Cricket's log.

D Lion made too much noise.

2 What caused Lion's ear to sting?

F Cricket was yelling at him.

G Mosquito was buzzing in it.

H Lion was shaking his head.

J Lion was scratching his ear.

3 What was the effect of Lion's meeting with Mosquito?

A Lion ran away.

B Lion threatened Cricket.

C Lion slapped Mosquito.

D Lion challenged Cricket.

4 How would you describe the change in Lion at the end of the story?

F He became less boastful.

G He became less patient.

H He became more foolish.

J He became more angry.

5 Why do you think people would enjoy a story about a cricket who chased away a lion?

_____

_____

_____

_____

_____

_____

Name _____

Read the selection. Then answer the questions that follow.

The Spider Tower

The Zuni people of the Southwest tell an ancient story about a spider who saved a hunter. The hunter was in the desert when suddenly a group of men from another tribe came upon him. They told him he could not hunt on their land, though the desert did not belong to anyone at that time. They chased him into a deep canyon. Outnumbered, the hunter did not want to argue. He looked for a way to escape. He came to a tall narrow pillar of rock. It rose hundreds of feet above the canyon floor like a tower.

The hunter thought that the sides of the tower were too smooth to climb. As he got closer, he realized that a rope hung down from the top. As his pursuers drew near, the hunter grabbed the rope and climbed. When he reached the top, he gathered up the rope.

The hunter was exhausted by the time he reached the summit of the tower. He collapsed and rested. He could hear the men below. Even when it sounded as if they'd left, he stayed for days, drinking rainwater and eating birds' eggs.

When he felt safe again and was about to leave, he suddenly wondered where the rope had come from. He followed it to a huge, strong spider web. In the center of the web sat the spider, who had seen his plight and saved him.

The hunter thanked the spider and then used the rope to descend to the canyon floor and return home safely.

Turn the page.

Answer the questions below.

1 Why did the group of men chase the hunter into the canyon?

  A They hoped to trap him there.

  B They knew there was a tower there.

  C They were afraid of him.

  D They were lost.

2 Why did the hunter begin to wonder where the rope had come from?

  F The rope started to move.

  G He knew that no one had ever climbed the tower.

  H He no longer had to worry about being pursued.

  J The rope had mysteriously disappeared.

3 Which of the following characterizes the main conflict in this story?

  A being allowed to hunt in the desert

  B being able to climb a tall rock tower

  C being able to survive on rainwater and birds' eggs

  D being allowed to meet the spider

4 Why did the hunter gather up the rope?

_____

_____

_____

_____

5 What is the most likely reason the hunter stayed on top of the tower for a few days?

_____

_____

_____

_____

Name _____

Read the selection. Then answer the questions that follow.

Melampus and the Snakes

Melampus was a boy who lived in ancient Greece. One day, a snake was killed near his home. Melampus felt sorry for the snake's two babies, so he took care of them and made them his pets. The little snakes did something for Melampus in return. They taught him to understand the languages of all the animals. And later, when Melampus grew up, that knowledge saved his life.

Some enemies captured Melampus and put him in jail. There were mice in the cell, and Melampus heard them talking. They told him that worms had eaten through the heavy beam in the ceiling, and it would soon crash down. Melampus asked his enemies to move him to another cell, which they did. The beam soon fell. Melampus's enemies were in awe of his wisdom, so they set him free.

Turn the page.

Answer the questions below.

1 **What is the theme of the story?**

A Snakes make good pets.

B Kindness is often repaid.

C Wise men make the best leaders.

D Never trust your enemies.

2 **Which time period could be the setting for the story?**

F 2,500 years ago

G 250 years ago

H 25 years ago

J The present

3 **From the setting of this story, you know that it is**

A an Indian legend.

B a Norse myth.

C a Greek myth.

D a French folk tale.

4 **Which part of the story is an event told out of order, and how does that add to the plot of the story?**

_____

_____

_____

_____

_____

_____

_____

_____

_____

Name _____

Read the selection. Then answer the questions that follow.

Best Friends

The island of Sicily lies in the Mediterranean Sea, south of Italy. In ancient times, a cruel king ruled the island. He punished people simply for saying things he did not like. The king had spies all over the island to make sure that no one spoke against him.

One day, a man named Pythias was speaking to his friend Damon. He said loudly, "The king is an evil man!" Immediately, the king's spies grabbed Pythias, and he and Damon were hauled away to the palace. The king sentenced Pythias to death.

"I accept my fate," Pythias said. "I ask only that you let me visit my family one last time."

"I will take his place in prison," Damon added, "and die in his place if he fails to return."

The king was sure that Pythias would leave Damon to die. Still, he was curious to see what would happen, so he agreed to the deal. Pythias had thirty days to return.

When the thirtieth day came, Pythias had not come back. The king told Damon that he had been a fool, but Damon said, "My friend is surely dead, or he would be here."

As the executioner led Damon away, Pythias arrived, bruised and battered.

"I'm so glad I arrived in time!" he gasped. "I was robbed and beaten, left without money or strength to get here. But I made it! Now my friend can live!"

The king of Sicily was moved by such loyalty and sacrifice. He allowed both Damon and Pythias to go free.

Turn the page.

Answer the questions below.

1 **What is the theme of the story?**

A Kings are cruel.

B Crimes are always punished.

C True friends are loyal.

D Speaking up is dangerous.

2 **Approximately which time period could be the setting for the story?**

F 2,500 years ago

G 250 years ago

H 25 years ago

J The present

3 **Where does the story take place?**

A in a prison

B in Italy

C on a ship

D on an island

4 **Why did Damon agree to stay in prison in Pythias's place?**

F He trusted Pythias to return.

G He wanted Pythias to live.

H He knew that Pythias would be robbed.

J He wanted to spy on the king.

5 **Why does it not seem possible for such a story to happen in a democracy?**

_____

_____

_____

_____

_____

_____

_____

Name _____

Read the selection. Then answer the questions that follow.

A King and a Conqueror

In ancient Greece, there was a town that needed a king. The people's gods had told them that their king would be a stranger who would arrive in town riding in a wagon. The people waited and waited, but their king did not come. Losing patience, all the people gathered to talk about their problem. Just then, a wagon rolled into town carrying a handsome young man.

The man's name was Gordius, and he was just a poor farmer looking for water for himself and his horse. Imagine his surprise when the people made him their king! When they explained to Gordius that they had recognized him as their leader because of his wagon, Gordius decided to make the wagon an object of honor. He parked it in the town square, tying it to a post with a very complicated knot to prevent it from being stolen.

The people were quite amazed by Gordius's knot. After a time, a legend began about the knot. It was said that whoever could untie Gordius's knot would rule all of Asia. Such a legend tempted many people to try to undo the knot, but no one succeeded.

A long time passed without much excitement in the town, and then another special visitor arrived: Alexander the Great, ruler of the Greek Empire. All the people held their breath when Alexander tried to untie Gordius's knot. He struggled with it but could not untangle it. Then, suddenly, Alexander drew his sword and cut the knot apart in one mighty swing. He left the town and went on to rule all of Asia.

Turn the page.

Answer the questions below.

1 **Which time period appears to be the setting for the story?**

   A 2,500 years ago

   B 250 years ago

   C 25 years ago

   D The present

2 **Which of these is the theme of the story?**

   F A weak man may be a great leader.

   G A farmer king is better than a warrior king.

   H Success may come from luck or strength.

   J Every knot can be untied.

3 **Which word best describes Alexander?**

   A foolish

   B cruel

   C determined

   D generous

4 **Based on the theme, how did each character become a leader?**

_____

_____

_____

_____

_____

5 **How might Gordius's arrival been different if the story had been set in a city by the sea?**

_____

_____

_____

_____

_____

Name _____

Read the selection. Then answer the questions that follow.

Care Means Growth

People think the best shade tree is an oak. But when it comes to planting a tree in their yards, they choose something else. They want a tree to grow practically overnight, like the beanstalk in a fairytale. People don't realize that how fast a tree grows depends on the quality of care it gets. With the right care, an oak can grow faster than you think.

Water deeply once a week, and keep the grass cleared from the base of the tree. Grass will use the "food" in the soil and the rainwater, thus slowing the tree's growth. Most people are too lazy to mulch. Mulching, which is the spreading of natural materials like leaves, grass clippings, or chipped bark around the base, controls grass and weeds.

Turn the page.

Answer the questions below.

1 **Which sentence from the selection includes both a statement of fact and a statement of opinion?**

A But when it comes to planting a tree in their yards, they choose something else.

B People don't realize that how fast a tree grows depends on the quality of care it gets.

C Water deeply once a week, and keep the grass cleared from the base of the tree.

D They want a tree to grow practically overnight, like the beanstalk in a fairytale.

2 **Based on the passage, what happens when you let grass grow around the base of a tree?**

F It creates mulch to protect the tree's roots.

G It improves the growth of an oak tree.

H It uses food and water that the tree needs.

J It helps keep the weeds under control.

3 **Which sentence is a statement of opinion?**

A Water deeply once a week.

B Keep the grass cleared from the base of the tree.

C Most people are too lazy to mulch.

D Mulching around the base controls grass and weeds.

4 **The author writes that people "want a tree to grow practically overnight, like the beanstalk in a fairytale." Based on this statement, what do you think is the author's opinion of these types of gardeners?**

_____

_____

_____

_____

_____

_____

_____

_____

Name _____

Read the selection. Then answer the questions that follow.

Little Man, Big Voice

If you haven't yet heard of Dalton Sherman, you should soon. Dalton, a fifth grader at Charles Rice Learning Center, spoke at Dallas's August 2008 school rally to nearly *twenty thousand* people. Those in the audience, mostly teachers, but also parents and students, hung on his every word. They responded by clapping, nodding, smiling, and even shouting. Dalton's message to Dallas teachers was simple: *Believe in yourselves, believe in each other, and believe in your students.*

Dalton's family clearly believes in him. His grandmother says that he, like President Barack Obama, has the "it" factor. Her hopes for Dalton are no higher than Dalton's own hopes for himself. "I'm in it to win it," Dalton says, though his own goals don't keep him from caring about his listeners. "When I hear them cheering," he says, "it's like, 'Oh yeah, they're feeling me!'"

Dalton impressed a lot of people at the rally in Dallas. Since that skilled performance, people all over the nation have begun to hear about Dalton. Some people grumble that he is not really as talented as people believe. They think that his teachers helped him too much. For example, they point out, he did not compose his own speech. Two teachers did. Teachers also helped him practice and prepare for its delivery. Supporters of Dalton point out that many famous historic figures did not write their own speeches either. Public speaking is its own art, and, writer or not, Dalton is an artist.

Turn the page.

Answer the questions below.

1 **Which sentence from the selection is a statement of fact?**

A If you haven't yet heard of Dalton Sherman, you should soon.

B Those in the audience, mostly teachers but also parents and students, hung on his every word.

C They responded by clapping, nodding, smiling, and even shouting.

D Public speaking is its own art, and, writer or not, Dalton is an artist.

2 **What opinion is shown by the emphasis the author puts on the phrase *"twenty thousand"* in the second sentence of the selection?**

F Attendance at the rally was lower than expected.

G The place was far too crowded for people to hear very well.

H The size of the audience made Dalton feel afraid.

J Being asked to speak before such a big crowd was an honor.

3 **Based on the selection, which statement *best* describes the effect that Dalton's public speaking has on his listeners?**

A Most people who hear Dalton think he is cheating.

B People disagree about what Dalton has achieved so far.

C All people who hear Dalton are impressed by him.

D Some people think Dalton is writing his own speeches.

4 **The author writes, "Some people grumble that he is not really as talented as people believe." Based on the selection, which clue word in this sentence shows the author's opinion of this statement?**

F grumble

G really

H talented

J believe

5 **The author's stated opinion is that "Public speaking is its own art." How is this opinion meant to defend Dalton?**

_____

_____

_____

_____

Name _____

Read the selection. Then answer the questions that follow.

Cell Phones and Schools

By now you're used to seeing people of all ages walking, shopping, or even driving with a cell phone attached to one ear. Now imagine students, in class, each gazing into a cell phone's display screen to do an assignment. In fact, fifth graders in several schools are doing that. The phones, which hold special software designed by Professor Elliot Soloway, are part of a learning experiment.

Every student needs a computer, Soloway believes, and in the future that computer will be a cell phone. "The cell phone," he says, "is now as essential as a pair of shoes or a coat." At the recent Mobile Learning Conference in Washington, supporters of the experiment argued that cell phones are cheaper and more portable than laptops, which often have to be wheeled from class to class on a cart.

Text messaging and dialing were disabled on the phones donated for the experiment. Students can access the Internet, use a calculator, take pictures and make videos, write reports, and send information to each other. At Trinity Meadows Intermediate School in Texas, students photographed the hallway with their phones. They measured the length and width of the hallway and used their phones to calculate its area. In a classroom nearby, students used their phones to do online research for a history lesson.

Some teachers consider cell phones more of a distraction than a learning tool. But that kind of thinking, Soloway believes, can't stop technology.

Turn the page.

Answer the questions below.

1 **Which sentence includes a statement of opinion?**

A The phones, which hold software designed by Professor Elliot Soloway, are part of a learning experiment.

B Every student needs a computer, Soloway believes, and in the future that computer will be a cell phone.

C Students can access the Internet, use a calculator, take pictures and make videos, write reports, and send information to each other.

D At Trinity Meadows Intermediate School in Texas, students photographed the hallway with their phones.

2 **For the experiment, changes were made to the cell phones for the students. What effect did those changes have on the way the cell phones could be used?**

F The phones could not take any videos or photographs.

G The phones had more memory for other programs.

H The students could not dial calls or send text messages.

J The students had to use the full spellings of words.

3 **The author writes, "Some teachers consider cell phones more of a distraction than a learning tool." Which of these would be the *best* way to find out if this statement of fact is correct?**

A asking a teacher how often he or she uses a cell phone in daily life

B taking a cell phone to school and trying to use it during class to do research

C writing Professor Soloway to ask how his cell-phone software works

D contacting teachers at Trinity Meadow to ask how they feel about cell phones

4 **From the information in the selection, can you tell which opinion the author *most likely* favors: are cell phones a distraction or a learning tool? Explain your answer.**

_____

_____

_____

5 **Professor Soloway states that a cell phone is "as essential as a pair of shoes or a coat." Explain what his statement of opinion means.**

_____

_____

_____

Name _____

Read the selection. Then answer the questions that follow.

Tough Cookies

Making cookies? Stick to these rules and your cookies will be great!

- Use room-temperature butter, or it will not blend correctly with the sugar. Set it out at least one hour ahead. It should be soft but not separating or melting.

- Dry ingredients like flour and sugar should be measured in dry measuring cups, never in liquid cups. Flour does not need to be sifted before measuring unless the recipe says so. If a recipe calls for sifted flour, make sure to sift, even if the flour is labeled "pre-sifted."

- For liquids, use a marked plastic or glass measuring cup. The measuring cup should have space above the one-cup line to prevent spilling. To get a correct reading, set the cup on a flat surface before checking the level.

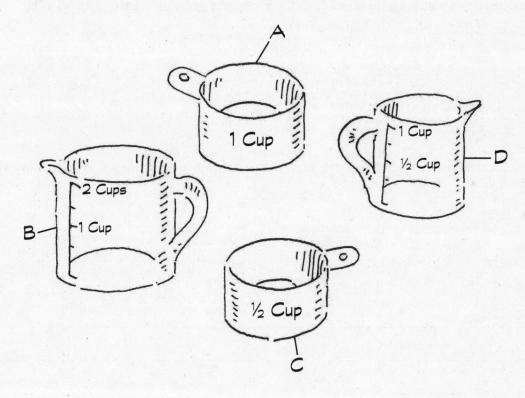

Turn the page.

Answer the questions below.

1 What causes butter to separate?

A baking

B blending

C time

D temperature

2 Using flour with "pre-sifted" on its label could lead a baker to make what mistake?

F The baker might use it when sugar is called for.

G The baker might measure it with a glass measuring cup.

H The baker might think it never needs to be sifted.

J The baker might mix it with too much melted butter.

3 What would *most likely* happen if you were to forget to set a glass measuring cup on a flat surface before checking the level of its contents?

A You would get less or more liquid than you needed.

B You would prevent the flour in it from settling correctly.

C You would mix up the flour and sugar incompletely.

D You would spill some liquid because it is right at the top.

4 Look at the illustrations. Which two kinds of cups are best for measuring liquid? Explain how you know.

_____

_____

_____

_____

_____

_____

_____

_____

Name _____

Read the selection. Then answer the questions that follow.

The Tender Rose

Roses, like humans, can get sick. They can be infected by funguses, viruses, mites, and bacteria. Some of these ailments are contagious to other roses, and some are even deadly.

Common fungal diseases include black spot, downy mildew, powdery mildew, and rust. Wet weather, humidity, and poor air circulation (being planted too close to a wall, for example) encourage fungal disease. Black spot shows up on the oldest leaves first, appearing as black spots surrounded by yellow zones. Downy mildew appears as purple blotches on the leaves, which turn yellow and drop. Both of these funguses weaken the canes (branches) and can kill a rose bush. Powdery mildew looks like fuzzy white powder on the leaves. The leaves curl, ripple, or fold closed, and buds form poorly if at all. Rust makes the leaves look rusted on the underside along their spines. The leaves turn yellow, then brown, and then drop off. Some types of roses catch rust easily and can die from it.

These funguses are spread in similar ways. Spores form on wet leaves. Watering or rain splashes the spores around, or wind transports them to other plants. Spores can also travel on pruning tools and on hands, although they are harmless to humans.

Keeping a rose healthy requires planting it in an airy spot, putting mulch (bark chips) around its base, and regularly watering the ground around it, not the bush itself, to avoid water lingering on the leaves.

ROSE AILMENTS			
DISEASE	WEATHER	SYMPTOMS	EFFECTS
Black spot	Hot, humid, poor air circulation	Black spots, yellow zones surrounding them, on oldest leaves first	Leaves drop, weak canes, possible death
Downy mildew	Cool, damp weather	Purple blotches on leaves, leaves turn yellow, purplish black spots on canes	Leaves drop suddenly, infected canes die over winter
Powdery mildew	Damp weather, shade, poor circulation	Fuzzy white powder on leaves and stems	Curled or rippled leaves, leaves that fold closed, poor bud development
Rust	Warm, wet weather, poor air circulation	Orange growths on undersides of leaves; leaves turn yellow	Leaves turn yellow, then brown, then drop; possible death in some roses

Turn the page.

Answer the questions below.

1 Based on the selection, what condition would make it easier for a fungus to infect a rose?

   A watering the ground around the roots

   B getting a long stretch of sunny, dry weather

   C having brief rains followed by warm sun

   D planting in a corner right next to the house

2 Which of the following *best* describes the effect of the rust fungus on roses?

   F deadly to almost all roses

   G harmless to most roses

   H deadly to some roses

   J harmful to few roses

3 Based on information in the selection, if the weather is sunny and there is no wind, what *most likely* happens to spores?

   A They stay just where they are.

   B They multiply quickly.

   C They start to hurt humans.

   D They splash all around.

4 Look at the table of information. How are the effects of powdery mildew *different* from those of the other funguses?

   F The leaves drop suddenly instead of turning yellow first.

   G The fungus damages the leaves, but they do not drop.

   H The roses with the fungus are able to bloom normally.

   J The fungus bothers only the oldest, weakest canes.

5 Basing your answer upon the information in the last paragraph, tell what part of rose care you think people would *most often* forget. Explain why you think that would happen.

_____

_____

_____

_____

_____

Name _____

Read the selection. Then answer the questions that follow.

The Moth and the Flower

The hawk moth and the datura plant have what scientists call a "mutual" relationship, one that benefits both species. These types of relationships in nature have long fascinated scientists, in part because this kind of cooperation seems so complex and weirdly human. One partner in this type of relationship often seems to benefit more, which makes scientists especially curious.

Each large, trumpet-shaped datura flower blooms only for one night. The flowers begin to open at twilight, and their strong lemony scent draws the hawk moths. The hawk moth is as big as a man's hand. It drinks nectar from the flower and, while on it, transfers the pollen that enables the flower to create seeds. The female hawk moth deposits her eggs on the gray-green datura leaves. The caterpillars hatch and eat the leaves down to nubs. The plant pays a high price for having its pollen moved!

Scientists did an experiment to study what effect the moths' behavior has on the root system of the datura plants. In each pair of test plants, the first plant was protected from hawk moth caterpillars. The second plant was exposed to them. Scientists learned that root growth in the plants exposed to the caterpillars slowed because the plant had to use energy to make new leaves, which were not as healthy as the originals.

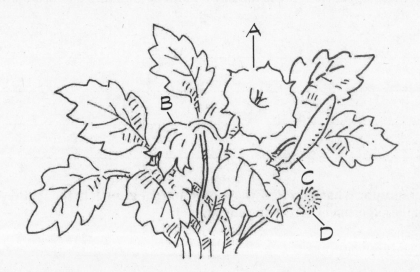

Turn the page.

Answer the questions below.

1 According to the selection, which feature of "mutual" relationships produces the *most* curiosity among scientists?

A Each partner gains something from the arrangement.

B The connection resembles a very weird friendship.

C One partner appears to receive much greater benefits.

D The interaction affects the growth of both partners.

2 What happens to draw the hawk moths to the datura plant?

F The eggs on its gray-green leaves fascinate them.

G The trumpet-like shape of the blooms attracts them.

H The strong scent of the blossoms appeals to them.

J The pollen inside the flowers provides food for them.

3 Look at the drawing. Which feature shows that it must be night-time?

A feature A

B feature B

C feature C

D feature D

4 Describe two events that happened because the hawk moth caterpillars hatched on the datura plant.

_____

_____

_____

5 Re-read the last paragraph. What *most likely* happened to root growth in the first datura plant of the pairs used in the experiment? Explain your answer.

_____

_____

_____

_____

Name _____

Read the selection. Then answer the questions that follow.

Letter from Camp

Dear Belinda,

Greetings from camp! I'm having a great time. Believe it or not, I get up even earlier than we do during the school year. I don't mind though, because here I wake up in my bunk in a cabin in the woods. I hear the sounds of birds instead of the sounds of cars whizzing by my house. We go hiking and swimming and do crafts. I am learning how to make ink and paint from berries and wild flowers. Painting is still my favorite thing to do. Last night one of the counselors taught us about the stars. We learned how to spot the North Star and the Big Dipper. I can see millions more stars here than I can at home.

I hope you're having a fun summer. Write me a letter and tell me about it.

Your friend,

Maria

Turn the page.

Answer the questions below.

1 How does Maria's home differ from camp?

A Home is in the city.

B Home is quieter.

C Home is near the woods.

D Home has bunk beds.

2 How does the sky at camp differ from the sky at home?

F It has fewer clouds.

G It is darker.

H Maria sees more birds in it.

J Maria sees more stars in it.

3 What does Maria do at camp that she probably also enjoys doing at home?

A hiking

B swimming

C cooking

D painting

4 Why do you think Maria wrote the letter to Belinda?

_____

_____

_____

_____

_____

_____

_____

_____

_____

_____

Name _____

Read the selection. Then answer the questions that follow.

Letter to a Friend

Dear Eric,

Well, school started last week. Finally, I am in sixth grade. I go to a different school. One benefit is that it starts later than my elementary school, so I don't have to get up so early. Of course, this year, instead of being one of the oldest students, I'm one of the youngest. Our middle school has sixth, seventh, and eighth grades.

I can tell already that school will be more challenging this year. I had homework the very first day! Instead of recess, we have study hall. I think science will still be my favorite subject. The science lab has a lot of cool equipment, from microscopes to telescopes. Besides studying cells and constellations, we also get to do chemistry experiments.

Wish me luck: I'm going to try out for the track team again. Since this is my first year here, I may not make the team, but I decided to try anyway. I found out that there is a chess club. My aunt taught me to play chess over the summer, and I really like it. I think I will try the club out and test my skills!

One thing that never seems to change, no matter where you go to school, is the cafeteria. The plastic chairs, the fish sticks, the French fries, that slimy green stuff they call spinach—it's all strangely familiar. The only good thing I can say about it is that at least it's the one thing I'm already used to!

I know you can't wait to get to sixth grade, but next year will be here before you know it.

Your friend,

Tony

Turn the page.

Answer the questions below.

1 How did Tony's new school differ from his old school?

  A It started earlier.

  B It taught science.

  C It had a track team.

  D It had study hall.

2 How was Tony different from most students at his new school?

  F He was younger.

  G He was smarter.

  H He had more homework.

  J He ran faster.

3 What part of Tony's day at his new school was most like his old school?

  A recess

  B lunchtime

  C physical education

  D chess club

4 How did the ages of the two boys compare?

  F Eric was about a year older than Tony.

  G Tony was about a year older than Eric.

  H Eric was two years older than Tony.

  J They were the same age.

5 Why do you think Tony wrote the letter to Eric?

_____

_____

_____

_____

_____

_____

Name _____

Read the selection. Then answer the questions that follow.

Letter from a Pen Pal

Dear Lisa,

Greetings from India! I was thrilled to receive your letter and hear about your life in Chicago. I have never been to the United States, but my brother resides in Houston, and I hope to visit him soon.

Since you said that you have never been to India, I will tell you a little bit about this vast country. We have two seasons, the monsoon season and the dry season. During the monsoon season, it rains almost all the time. During the dry season, rain is altogether absent. If either season lasts too long, it is very bad for farmers such as my parents. The temperature varies from one time of year to another, but not nearly as much as it does in Chicago. I cannot envision what your city is like in the winter, with the freezing wind blowing snow in all directions and slick ice covering the ground. (By the way, it never gets cold enough to snow in the region of India where I live. It does snow high in the Himalayan Mountains to the north, however.) If you lived where I live, you would say that it is summer all the time.

You wrote about American movies. Many Indians love to go to the movies too. India has a thriving movie industry, and new films are released every week. However, most Indians have never tried rollerskating or bowling, and we play cricket instead of baseball.

Here is something about my country that might surprise you: English is one of its official languages, along with Hindi. Please respond and tell me more about your life in the United States.

Your friend,

Sanjay

Turn the page.

Answer the questions below.

1 Which of the following is more popular in India than it is in the United States?

  A movies

  B bowling

  C cricket

  D baseball

2 What does the letter indicate that Sanjay and Lisa have in common?

  F They live in big cities.

  G They speak English.

  H They like American movies.

  J They like winter.

3 How does the climate in India differ from the climate in Chicago?

  A Temperatures are more extreme in India.

  B Temperatures are warmer in India.

  C India does not have droughts.

  D India has no snow.

4 Sanjay and Lisa are pen pals who appear not to have met in real life. Based on Sanjay's response to Lisa's letter, what personality traits do they seem to have in common?

_____

_____

_____

_____

5 What does Sanjay focus on in his letter?

_____

_____

_____

_____

_____

Name _____

Read the selection. Then answer the questions that follow.

Planting a Grafted Rose

Many roses are hard to grow because they have a weak root structure. Therefore, when these roses are young, each is *grafted* onto the root of a stronger rose. The joint is called the *union*.

To plant a grafted rose, dig a hole that is about two feet wide and two feet deep. Put organic compost in the bottom, add soil, and build a little mound. Make sure that, when the rose sits on the mound, its roots have plenty of room to trail over without hitting the sides. The union, or grafted joint, must be one to two inches below the soil line. As you would for any rose, fill in the hole with rich soil and press it down to get rid of air pockets. Water well and put mulch over the soil.

Turn the page.

Answer the questions below.

1 When do you add compost to the hole in which a rose is to be planted?

   A After watering the plant

   B Once the roots are arranged

   C Before building a soil mound

   D Right after pressing down the soil

2 When you are planting a rose, when do you add the layer of mulch?

   F You put it at the bottom of the hole recently dug.

   G You make it trail over the sides of the little mound.

   H You press it down two inches below the soil line.

   J You apply it last on top of the rich, watered soil.

3 Based on information in the passage, what is the *main difference* between a rose on its own root and a rose grafted onto the root of a stronger rose?

   A The grafted rose's roots are arranged around a mound of soil.

   B The grafted rose requires a bigger hole.

   C The rose on its own root is planted without touching the sides.

   D The rose on its own root has no union.

4 Describe in the correct order the five major steps of planting a rose. Base your answer on information in the selection.

_____

_____

_____

_____

_____

_____

_____

_____

Name _____

Read the selection. Then answer the questions that follow.

A Floating Palace

Imagine the magical white world of the Antarctic. Snow compresses under its own weight on the upper part of glaciers. It begins a slow slide downhill to the sea. Tongues of ice and snow build on the surface of the water. Over time, wind and waves wear at these tongues. Seawater temperatures can grow warm enough to melt the underside of the ice shelf, causing it to become unstable. Large fractures appear in the ice shelf. These fractures can extend hundreds of miles. Over time these fractures can cause blocks of ice to break off suddenly in a process called "calving." This is how icebergs are born, after which they are carried away by the ocean current.

Through this natural cycle, the edge of the ice shelf is extended by ice flow, moved back when icebergs break away, and then extended again. It's a slow cycle. It can take up to twenty years or longer for a tongue of ice to break and send an iceberg on its way.

Many explorers have been enchanted by the sight of icebergs adrift on the tossing sea. They have compared the icebergs to pyramids, churches, and palaces. Some are huge, towering hundreds of feet above the surface. Their white color results from small pockets of gas spread throughout the ice. In sunny weather, as the surface of an iceberg melts, water streams in twinkling waterfalls over ledges of its jagged face.

Turn the page.

Answer the questions below.

1 While seawater is melting the underside of the tongues of ice, what is happening to the top of them?

A Snow is compressing them.

B They are towering over the sea.

C Wind is wearing them down.

D They are drifting on the ocean.

2 The selection compares an iceberg to

F a tongue.

G a slide.

H a church.

J a waterfall.

3 Based on the selection, which of the following *best* describes the sequence of natural changes to the ice shelf over a period of about 30 years?

A The shelf breaks off closer and closer to the glaciers.

B The shelf extends outward and then breaks off.

C The shelf shrinks in some places and breaks in others.

D The shelf keeps going farther on the ocean surface.

4 The author describes how icebergs are born. Where in the selection would it be *best* to include additional information about the dangers of icebergs to ships?

F as a new first paragraph

G in the first paragraph

H as a new second paragraph

J in the third paragraph

5 Describe what you think will happen *next* to the icebergs. Base your answer on information given in the selection.

_____

_____

_____

_____

Name _____

Read the selection. Then answer the questions that follow.

Worth the Effort

Last weekend, I attended my cousin's graduation from medical school. Many people do not realize how much education a person needs to become a doctor. After Diana graduated from high school, she went to college for four years. Only then did she begin medical school. That took another four years, and it was hard. Diana took mostly science classes, and she studied all the time.

Our whole family is proud of Diana. She is a physician now. Yet, she still has more to learn. She will spend the next few years being what is called a *resident*. A resident is a physician who recently finished medical school and is getting on-the-job training while working with more experienced doctors. Even after she has finished being a resident, Diana will take continuing education classes from time to time so that she can learn about new ideas in health care.

On my fourth birthday, my mom had a party for me. Diana could not come because she had to study for a test. That memory reminded me just how long Diana has worked to make her dream come true. At her graduation, I asked Diana if it was worth all the hard work, and she said yes. I think that Diana is a wonderful example for anyone who wants to have a demanding career. She has inspired me to set high goals for myself and to work hard to reach them. I hope that she has inspired you too. If you have a dream of achieving something special, you should go all out to make your dream come true. It will be worth the effort.

Turn the page.

Answer the questions below.

1 Which of the following events would fall *last* on a time line of the story?

A Diana gets on-the-job training as a resident.

B Diana graduates from the medical school.

C Diana takes continuing education classes.

D Diana says it was worth all the hard work.

2 According to the passage, when did Diana take mostly science classes?

F while getting on-the-job training

G during high school

H while being a resident physician

J during medical school

3 Where is Diana at the time that the selection is being written?

A between medical school and being a resident

B at her graduation from medical school

C studying for an important science test

D in college preparing for medical school

4 What is the difference between Diana's effect on the speaker and Diana's effect on readers of the selection?

_____

_____

_____

_____

_____

5 Which part of the selection is an event told out of order? How can you tell?

_____

_____

_____

_____

Name _____

Read the selection. Then answer the questions that follow.

Fog on the Coast of Maine

Some people say that England has the thickest fog in the world. Don't tell that to the folks up in Maine though. They say that their fog is so thick you can drive a nail into it, and they have a story to prove it.

On a day too foggy for fishing, a fisherman decided to put new shingles on his roof. Bob started nailing down new shingles early in the morning, and at dark he was still nailing. Meanwhile, Bob's wife, Nellie, was inside sewing. Finally Bob went in for dinner and told Nellie, "I never knew what a castle we live in. I nailed shingles all day and never ran out of roof."

Nellie knew that she wasn't living in a castle, so she took a lantern outside and looked up. Bob had finished the roof before noon. After that he had been nailing shingles to the fog!

Turn the page.

Answer the questions below.

1 **According to the story, how are England and Maine alike?**

A Both are very cold.

B Both have thick fog.

C Both have storytellers.

D Both have fishermen.

2 **How was Nellie different from Bob?**

F She preferred being outdoors.

G She jumped to conclusions.

H She did not like to fish.

J She thought logically.

3 **Which two things happened at the same time?**

A Fog rolled in and Bob went fishing.

B Bob nailed shingles and Nellie sewed.

C Nellie held the lantern and Bob made dinner.

D Nellie went outside and Bob nailed shingles.

4 **How is this story different from a true story about fog?**

_____

_____

_____

_____

_____

_____

_____

_____

Name _____

Read the selection. Then answer the questions that follow.

Paul Bunyan and the First Parade

You may have heard of Paul Bunyan and his blue ox, Babe, but you probably have not heard how Paul and Babe led the first parade.

Paul was a logger. Each year, when all the nearby trees had been cut, the loggers had to move and build a new camp. That took a lot of time. Paul knew there had to be a better way. Then one winter day, Paul saw a group of children sledding.

That night around the fire, Paul told the other loggers about his plan. He asked Ollie, the blacksmith, if he could make some very large sled runners. Ollie said he could. Paul asked Danny, the best builder of them all, if he could attach those runners to the bottom of a building. Danny said he could. That was all Paul needed. He himself could lift the buildings onto the runners, and Babe could pull the buildings to the new camp. Only one man said Paul's plan wouldn't work, and that was Grumpy Gus, who never thought anything would turn out.

Ollie went to work on the runners right away. When the first snow began to fall, Paul and Danny went into action, turning the logging camp buildings into giant sleds. Ollie had also made a super-sized chain. Paul used it to chain all the buildings together. Finally, he hooked the chain to Babe's harness and yelled, "Ho, Babe!" Babe loved a good game and didn't need any help, but Paul and all the loggers helped him pull anyway. Townspeople all along the way turned out to cheer and wave as the logging camp paraded by.

Turn the page.

Answer the questions below.

1 How was Paul Bunyan different from the other loggers?

  A He came up with new ideas.

  B He preferred games to logging.

  C He believed his plan would work.

  D He took time off to go sledding.

2 How was the logging camp like a parade?

  F An ox was in the lead.

  G A band played.

  H The buildings passed by like floats.

  J People ran alongside the giant sleds.

3 When did Paul get his idea about moving the camp?

  A when he saw a parade

  B when he saw children sledding

  C as he sat by the fire

  D when Ollie made giant runners

4 How did Gus differ from the other loggers?

  F He was afraid of Babe.

  G He rarely did any work.

  H He did not support Paul's plan.

  J He stayed at the old camp.

5 How is this story probably different from a true story about a logging camp?

_____

_____

_____

_____

_____

_____

_____

Name _____

Read the selection. Then answer the questions that follow.

The Riverboat Race

In the days before cars and airplanes, the Mississippi River was a highway for riverboats carrying passengers and freight. Riverboat travel had its risks. A boat could hit a submerged rock or log and spring a leak. Boats sometimes ran into each other. But riverboating was also fun. Boats sometimes raced, with everyone on board cheering.

One spring, a young man from Missouri took his first riverboat trip. He was going to New Orleans, at the river's mouth, to sell the fine lumber his father had sent along with him. Peter was a serious young man with no taste for adventure. He warned the captain that there was to be no racing while he was aboard. The captain knew he might lose his job if the young man complained to the riverboat company, so he promised not to race.

A few days later, Peter was strolling on the deck when another riverboat streaked past. The crew on the passing boat called out to the crew of his, calling them slowpokes and turtles. Peter ran to the captain's quarters, where he took back his previous words and urged the captain to race.

"They've taken on extra wood," the captain said. "They've got a big, hot fire in their boiler, and I'm not sure we can match them."

Peter offered the captain some of his father's fine lumber to stoke the fire, and the race was on. Peter knew he would have to pay his father for the lumber the riverboat ate, but he didn't mind when his boat passed the other and the captain and crew gave a cheer.

Turn the page.

Answer the questions below.

1 How was Peter different at the end of the story than he was at the beginning?

A He was more adventurous.

B He was more patient.

C He was less sure of himself.

D He was less friendly.

2 Which word describes Peter both at the beginning of the story and at the end?

F careless

G foolish

H responsible

J generous

3 When did Peter decide to offer the captain some of his lumber?

A before he left home

B when the other boat passed his

C after he asked the captain to race

D when the captain and crew cheered

4 What detail of this story would probably be different if it were set in the present time?

_____

_____

_____

_____

5 In terms of sportsmanship, how did the crew of the other boat appear to be different from that of Peter's boat?

_____

_____

_____

_____

Name _____

Read the selection. Then answer the questions that follow.

Summer Wins

Summer is much better than winter. The weather is warm and almost always sunny. There are many fun things to do outside. I can bike with friends, go to a park, and maybe even go swimming. I also get to play soccer and attend baseball games. Summer is an ideal time to participate in sports or watch local teams compete. It occasionally rains in the summer, but summer thunderstorms usually don't last long.

Winter is cold, with little to do outside. Blizzards and icy roads make it difficult to go anywhere. If it snows you can go sledding, which is fun, but after a while you get chilled and your clothes grow wet and feel heavy. In winter, you often find yourself wishing for summer to return. Fortunately, it's on its way!

Turn the page.

Answer the questions below.

1 Based on information in the selection, how are winter and summer *alike*?

  A Some type of outdoor fun is possible during both seasons.

  B In each season, you find yourself wishing for the other.

  C You can participate in baseball and soccer in both seasons.

  D In each season, the storms do not last very long at all.

2 The author writes about something fun to do outside in winter. Why do you think the author *most likely* does this?

  F to generalize that people want to have fun in every season

  G to entertain readers with images of chilly children in wet coats

  H to conclude that winter really is every bit as good as summer

  J to show readers that his or her viewpoint is balanced and fair

3 The author writes about summer thunderstorms. Why do you think the author does this?

  A to describe how beautiful the thunder and the lightning are

  B to complain that the weather in the summer is far from perfect

  C to argue that wet clothes dry faster in summer than in winter

  D to show that summer weather delays fun activities only briefly

4 Based on this selection, what argument do you think the author would likely use to try to persuade you that fall is better than spring? Explain your answer.

_____

_____

_____

_____

_____

_____

_____

_____

Name _____

Read the selection. Then answer the questions that follow.

Dig *This!*

Some gardeners grow things to look at, others grow things to eat, and some do both. In my family, Dad is the first kind of gardener, and Mom is the second. Everyone should do some kind of gardening. It's a great way to relax, connect with nature, and put your own touches on the plot of land you call home.

My dad added a variety of plants and trees to our yard, and he planned and built stone paths to wind among them. He brought in some large white boulders and heaved them around until they landed in just the right spots. We have the most stunning yard in the neighborhood! I never tell him this, but my favorite part of our yard is the tall pine tree that has resided here longer than we have. I like to sit under it on the carpet of fallen red needles and smell the sharp resin in the cracks of its bark.

Every summer my mom grows tomatoes, cucumbers, squash, peppers, spinach, lettuce, and other vegetables. Last year she put in a strawberry patch. A couple of years earlier, she planted a row of blueberry bushes along the back fence. I love the bright salads and sweet pies— oh my!

I enjoy both kinds of gardening, even though I sometimes complain about the work. You cannot just leave a garden of either type all on its own. Plants and even trees need regular care to thrive. In other words, gardening also teaches you about care and responsibility, which are good lessons for anyone.

Turn the page.

Answer the questions below.

1 **The two types of gardeners are *alike* in that they both**

A complain about how much work gardening requires.

B try to get their family and friends to learn to garden.

C care most about how the garden looks to neighbors.

D devote time to planting and caring for their gardens.

2 **What does the author think that gardening provides?**

F a strong connection to your home

G a way to compete with neighbors

H a good time for problem-solving

J a lesson for people who eat meat

3 **What appears to be the author's favorite part of gardening with Mom?**

A admiring the garden's colors

B tending the vegetables

C eating food from the garden

D planting the bushes

4 **The author includes information about an old pine tree that Dad did not plant. Why do you think the author *most likely* does this?**

F To argue that the things from long ago bring us the most pleasure

G To show how certain parts of a garden can take on special meaning

H To explain that the yard looked fine before Dad started gardening

J To give an example of how large a tree can grow if it is tended to

5 **Based on the selection, which kind of gardening does the author think the reader should try?**

_____

_____

_____

_____

_____

_____

Name _____

Read the selection. Then answer the questions that follow.

Your Imagination "at Work"

My uncle Jack is a builder. He builds houses for people. Sometimes he takes me to the sites where the houses are being built. It's fascinating to see a house develop, step by step. It takes many different workers with different skills to get the job done. My uncle supervises plumbers, electricians, and other workers. I was sure I wanted to be a homebuilder like Uncle Jack, until he introduced me to an architect. An architect is the person who draws the plans that a builder follows to build a house.

I know I'd like coming up with a unique design for each individual house, using a computer to create and change pictures of its layout, and imagining how it would look in real life. Being that kind of artist would be satisfying. But I like working with people, and architects often work alone, indoors. Being a builder would allow me to be outside and deal with all kinds of people, but they would be working *for* me, not really *with* me. So there are things I would like, and things I would probably not like, about each of these careers.

Uncle Jack reminds me that, at the age of ten, I don't need to decide any time soon. Still, I think kids should imagine doing different things, like running a circus or even running the country! It's important to think about what goals you would need to achieve to get there.

Turn the page.

Answer the questions below.

1 In comparison to being a builder, being an architect seems

A lovely.

B lazy.

C lively.

D lonely.

2 In the first paragraph, which clue word does the author use to foreshadow mixed feelings about becoming a builder?

F takes

G supervises

H until

J follows

3 The author wants to persuade the reader to see different careers as

A hopelessly confusing.

B completely possible.

C generally frightening.

D probably mysterious.

4 Why does the author *most likely* speak of running a circus or running the country?

_____

_____

_____

_____

5 In this selection, the speaker considers whether to become a builder or an architect. What would you say would be *best* to do? Base your answer on the selection.

_____

_____

_____

_____

_____

_____

Name _____

Read the selection. Then answer the questions that follow.

Hats Off

I hated our art assignment, which was to decorate a hat to reflect our personality. Nothing about me seemed hat-like. I carried the plain starter hat home and stared at it.

"How about feathers?" my friend Tran asked. We were in a craft shop full of bells and feathers and buttons and other things that could be glued to a hat. "You like birds."

"I like *nature*," I said. "There's nothing natural about those orange feathers."

When I went to the pet supply store with my mother to pick up food for our dogs and cats, I wandered to the aquarium aisle.

I found great stuff—tiny divers and treasure chests, fantastic sea creatures. And the hat I made, with its seaweed and a little crab, showed my love of nature and the ocean.

Turn the page.

Answer the questions below.

1 What does the author use orange feathers to represent?

A fake nature

B colorful birds

C strong personalities

D big assignments

2 In the second and third paragraphs, the author includes a scene in a craft shop. Why do you think the author *most likely* includes this scene?

F to suggest that Tran is going to be making a hat too

G to show how poorly the art assignment fits the speaker

H to explain why shopping for feathers takes time

J to convince the reader it that hat-making is great fun

3 What is the theme of the story?

A Friends sometimes know us better than we know ourselves.

B Completing a task on time is as important as doing a good job.

C Most problems have a solution if you keep looking for one.

D The best things in life are those we discover while not looking.

4 Describe how the speaker feels about the art assignment once it is completed. Explain how the author's choice of details shows you this.

_____

_____

_____

_____

_____

_____

_____

_____

Name _____

Read the selection. Then answer the questions that follow.

At the Dog Park

Max and Maggie were flopped on the grass watching Roberta play with the red ball. She would run over to them, show them the ball, make excited noises to encourage them to get up and join her, and then run away from them.

"It's so cute when she plays with the ball alone," Maggie grinned.

"I play with her sometimes," Max sniffed defensively. "But my knees are creaky and it's hard on the hips. I wish we had that thick knotted rope. She sure does love tug-of-war."

Maggie stretched and yawned. It was so great at this park. In the other fenced area, the one open to multiple dogs, a squarely built little terrier yapped and chased a leggy blonde Labrador retriever. "A Lab would probably play ball with her," Maggie sighed.

"The last thing we need is another dog," Max snorted. He stood up and stretched. "I'll go do a few rounds of fetch so she gets enough exercise."

He jogged over to where Roberta was dashing back and forth with the ball and acted really excited to play with it. How surprised and happy she looked! How he loved her!

After playing some fetch, he dropped the ball and returned to where Maggie was lounging, eyes closed, in the sun. "Might be your turn," he hinted, nudging her.

"Nope," Maggie huffed and rolled over. "Actually, she looks ready to leave."

"Okay, you two sweet, lazy dogs," Roberta called, shaking her car keys. "We can go home!"

Turn the page.

Answer the questions below.

1 At the beginning of the story, the author tries to persuade the reader that

   A lonely Roberta has very few friends.

   B dogs get jealous of each other.

   C Roberta is Max and Maggie's dog.

   D dogs can talk to each other.

2 Readers understand from the clues about the setting that this story's characters

   F only see each other at this park.

   G come to this park together.

   H are at this park for the first time.

   J keep off the grass at this park.

3 Why do you think the author included the last paragraph?

   A to explain why the game of fetch must come to an end

   B to reveal that Roberta the dog is able to talk like a person

   C to show clearly that Roberta is the human in the story

   D to suggest that Max and Maggie are too old to have fun

4 What is the author's *main* purpose in this selection?

   F to entertain readers with a surprise twist to the usual dog story

   G to persuade people to take their dogs out to play at dog parks

   H to convince readers that everyone should have at least two dogs

   J to show people how dogs are talking to each other all the time

5 What does the author *most likely* want people to believe about dogs' feelings towards their human owners?

_____

_____

_____

_____

_____

_____

Name _____

Read the selection. Then answer the questions that follow.

Learning to See

My sister has some unusual ideas about babysitting. Last time she was keeping an eye on me, she took me to the mall. She purchased earplugs at a drugstore, led us to a comfortable bench, and sat me down next to her. Then she opened the package of earplugs and handed me a pair.

"We're going to stop hearing and just see for ten minutes," she said, "and then we'll tell each other what we saw."

Sounds silly, right? I watched a woman towing a little girl by the hand. The woman's expression was strident, her mouth working overtime. The kid was tilted backward, slowing their progress on purpose. I saw two teenagers in love. Well, one of them looked in love. The boy clung to the girl's hand and contemplated one side of her face. She gazed fiercely into every store window as if searching for an enemy in the bush. When she lunged toward a store, she nearly left her hand and the swooning boy behind her.

"I don't like this," I said to Geneva, who smiled and pointed at her earplugs. My voice sounded strange to me. I could feel everything everyone was feeling—the little girl, guilty but stubborn, her mother angry, the teenage girl bored and selfish, the teenage boy hurt and trying too hard. I took out my earplugs. "THERE'S TOO MUCH TO SEE," I said right beside my sister's ear.

"What?" she said, smiling again, taking out her earplugs.

Turn the page.

Answer the questions below.

1 At the start of paragraph 3, the author has the speaker say "Sounds silly, right?" in order to

A introduce some unexpected results.

B show you that the earplugs worked.

C persuade readers to avoid watching.

D explain why teenagers get so bored.

2 To show the teenage girl's feelings, the author compares her to

F a babysitter at the mall.

G a mother defending a child.

H a soldier out on patrol.

J a child who cannot hear things.

3 What is the theme of the story?

A We leap to false conclusions when we lack information.

B The imagination provides details that may not be true.

C Listening can reveal things that are not actually told aloud.

D Sometimes we can hear more clearly by using our eyes.

4 What is the *most likely* reason that the author chooses a mall for the setting of this story?

_____

_____

_____

5 Which detail does the author include to suggest that Geneva's watching experience *differs* from the speaker's?

_____

_____

_____

_____

_____

Name _____

Read the selection. Then answer the questions that follow.

Not Home Alone

Edward's mother was a writer. She had an office in their home, and she worked very hard. Writing takes a great deal of concentration.

One afternoon Edward's mother was busy writing, and Edward was on the couch in the next room reading a book.

All was going well until he heard a noise from the ceiling. Edward froze. Every part of his body became an ear. He looked into his mother's office. She was staring at the computer screen. Then he heard it again.

He got the broom and climbed the attic stairs. He peeked inside. The noise grew faster. It came from his drum set near the chimney.

As he looked more closely, he saw a squirrel with its paw wedged in a crack in the wood floor. Its tail was beating the drum. Edward prodded it with the broom, and then it was able to run off.

Later Edward's mother came out of her office. "What have you been reading?" she asked.

Edward smiled, "Sherlock Holmes. But I wasn't scared."

Turn the page.

Answer the questions below.

1 **Why did Edward look for the noise by himself?**

  A He thought he knew what it was.

  B He didn't want to disturb his mother.

  C He wanted to write a story about it.

  D He didn't think the noise was important.

2 **Which of the following happens *first*?**

  F A squirrel gets its paw stuck.

  G Edward looks into his mother's office.

  H A squirrel's tail beats a drum.

  J Edward's mother comes out of her office.

3 **What does Edward do *after* he prods the squirrel with a broom?**

  A He goes to look in his mother's office.

  B He moves his drums near the chimney.

  C He returns to his reading on the couch.

  D He sweeps up the rest of the attic floor.

4 **Identify the two main events of the story and tell what Edward's mother is doing when those events happen.**

_____

_____

_____

_____

_____

_____

_____

_____

Name _____

Read the selection. Then answer the questions that follow.

Scientist Marie Curie

Marie Curie was a child in Poland. Russia ruled over Poland at that time. One day when she went to school, soldiers stood by the door. That was the end of formal schooling for her in Poland. Curie, however, studied with a group of students and teachers in secret. They met in basements lit by candles.

To earn money, Curie worked as a domestic servant. She saved her wages to go to a university in Paris. While at the university, she discovered that her reading and mathematics skills were weak. So she spent most of her time studying those subjects. Curie tried hard and graduated at the top of her class. She earned diplomas in both mathematics and science.

She worked her way through school by doing tests in a lab. Later, as a scientist testing coal, she discovered a new element. She named it "polonium" after Poland. Curie also discovered radium. She found that radium destroyed diseased cells faster than it destroyed healthy cells. This fact became useful in treating certain diseases.

During her life, Curie worked very hard. She was awarded the famous Nobel Prize for her discoveries. She was the first woman to win it, and the first person to win it twice. Not bad for a girl who started out poor in reading and math!

Turn the page.

Answer the questions below.

1 **Why did Curie stop attending school when she was a child?**

A She belonged to a study club.

B She preferred studying in secret.

C Local schools were closed for repair.

D Soldiers kept students from attending school.

2 **Which event occurred *after* Curie graduated from a university?**

F Curie held a job in a lab doing scientific tests.

G Curie named an element "polonium" after Poland.

H Curie improved her reading and math skills.

J Curie secretly studied with students and teachers.

3 **At what point did Curie discover that her math and reading skills were weak?**

A as a servant earning money

B as a child in Poland

C as a scientist studying coal

D as a student in Paris

4 **Which two events in the selection happened *at the same time*?**

F Curie was living in Poland and working in a lab.

G Curie was studying math and discovering what radium could do.

H Curie was testing coal and discovering a new element.

J Curie was working as a servant and attending a university in Paris.

5 **About how old was Curie when she moved away from Poland? Explain your answer based on information in the selection.**

_____

_____

_____

_____

_____

_____

Name _____

Read the selection. Then answer the questions that follow.

From Tamales to Tired Chairs

With three generations present, the celebrations and reunions of Eduardo's family were big. The door would open and in would come a stream of people carrying beverages and food. On this day, he stood back and looked at his family.

His grandparents had always been old and had sat in the same tired chairs. His parents were like the people he watched on television. They joked about problems but never solved them. That made the shows funny, but not his own parents. Then there were his younger brothers and sisters and cousins. He didn't feel connected to them either. Fun for Eduardo meant playing video games and being online. He and his friends were the only ones who understood what was important.

As Eduardo watched his relatives, he noticed his uncle Beto, who stood silent through most family gatherings.

"Hey, Beto."

Beto tipped his head in greeting. Beto didn't waste words.

"This place is an anthill."

Again Beto tipped his head, meaning yes.

"How can we be family and all be so different?"

Beto looked at Eduardo for a very long moment. Finally, Beto the stone monument spoke. "You mean different from *you*."

Now Eduardo began using Beto's silent language. He nodded his head yes.

Beto smiled. "Yes, each generation is different, but each takes its turn carrying tamales. You're eleven years old. Now, go help your aunt."

Eduardo understood. "Each generation needs to be useful and helpful, and you can start small, by carrying tamales," Beto said.

Turn the page.

Answer the questions below.

1 What time period is Eduardo thinking about in the second paragraph of the selection?

A He imagines what future family gatherings would be like.

B He generalizes about the past family gatherings he has been to.

C He describes the family gathering he will be attending next.

D He explains how the people at the current gathering are related.

2 Eduardo stops speaking *right after*—

F Beto says each generation is different.

G he compares the gathering to an anthill.

H Beto replies to his first question.

J he says hello to his uncle Beto.

3 Why does Eduardo feel he is disconnected from his family members?

A He is hurt that his favorite relative, Beto, very rarely talks to him.

B He thinks everyone else likes tamales much more than he does.

C He is sad that his relatives cannot seem to solve their problems.

D He believes his friends are the only people who think like he does.

4 Eduardo's view of his family changes from the story's beginning to the story's end. Describe three stages in the way he sees them.

_____

_____

_____

_____

5 Eduardo "stood back and looked at his family." In what order did Eduardo think about his relatives?

_____

_____

_____

_____

Name _____

Read the selection. Then answer the questions that follow.

Green Me and Eggs

Ever since I can remember, I have hated eggs. I feel sick to my stomach thinking about eating them.

Eggs are a cell. Who would want to eat a cell? The egg has two parts: the yellow egg yolk and the drippy egg white. The yolk is a major source of vitamins and minerals. The egg white is a major source of protein. I turn green thinking about people eating eggs that aren't cooked hard. The white is sometimes like jelly in some parts.

My grandparents only eat egg whites. They whip them up and pretend they are eating the whole egg. They say our bodies need protein to be healthy. I'll find another food with protein.

If you are an egg eater, I'm happy for you. For me, facing an egg at breakfast would be the wrong way to start a day.

Turn the page.

Answer the questions below.

1 The speaker's refusal to have breakfast with an egg eater is based on

A opinions about eggs.

B opinions about those who eat eggs.

C facts about the nutrition in eggs.

D facts about how eggs should be cooked.

2 Which of the following best expresses the main idea of the selection?

F Eggs are a source of protein.

G The egg yolk is not good for you.

H The speaker does not like eggs.

J Most grandparents eat eggs.

3 In the selection, who provides evidence that the egg is a healthy food?

A the speaker's parents

B the speaker's grandparents

C a cook

D a friend

4 Give two reasons the speaker does not like eating eggs.

_____

_____

_____

_____

_____

_____

_____

_____

_____

Name _____

Read the selection. Then answer the questions that follow.

Strange Language

Ana, frustrated, went to her teacher after school. "Either English is a strange language or I am crazy. You don't say beefburger, you say hamburger, but there's no ham. What goes up when a car backs up?"

She continued excitedly, "Some words sound alike but are not spelled the same, like *two, to,* and *too.* Then there are words that look alike but are totally different, like *tear* and *tear.* Do I cry or rip my jacket?"

The teacher nodded at her to go on, so Ana did. "English spelling is very difficult since there are silent letters. Take for example, *cushion, dumb, eighth,* and *hymn.* Some words have two or more letters that make a different sound than they do alone, like in *phone* and *laugh.* The letter *a* has many different sounds: *apple, father, ape.* It is nearly impossible to learn!"

"I know it's hard," the teacher agreed. "Try thinking of it this way. The English language you are learning is like the United States, which is made up of different people from different places all over the world. They brought words with them. We have words like *patio* and *plaza* from Spanish and *avenue* and *gauge* from French. The language contains words as varied as the people, and it takes time to get to know many of them."

Ana smiled and said, "I'll keep trying."

Turn the page.

Answer the questions below.

1 Which of the following is a fact that Ana shared with her teacher?

A English is strange.

B English is hard to learn.

C English uses words from Spanish and French.

D In English, we say don't say beefburger.

2 Which of the following is the main focus of the selection?

F Ana's feelings

G the nature of the English language

H the work it takes to learn a language

J languages in general

3 Based on the selection, which of the following features of English does not frustrate Ana?

A spelling

B pronunciation

C word meanings

D grammar rules

4 How does the teacher treat Ana's confusion over English?

F with understanding

G with suspicion

H with humor

J with anger

5 What does the sentence "Do I cry or rip my jacket?" show about the English language?

_____

_____

_____

_____

_____

_____

Name _____

Read the selection. Then answer the questions that follow.

A Whale of a Problem

For ages, whales have swum the Earth's oceans. Every winter, thousands of Pacific Gray whales swim from Alaska to Mexico. They spend the summer feeding and swimming in the arctic food-rich waters. In December they swim south at five knots, or about five miles per hour. Until March they live in the warm waters off Mexico. Tourists love to watch them off the Mexico seashore. They are easy to spot since whales swim twenty-four hours a day, and Pacific Grays are forty to fifty feet long weighing fifty thousand to sixty thousand pounds.

Every year these whales breed, give birth, and raise their calves in the lagoons off the coast of Mexico. These lagoons, however, have been threatened by a salt company wanting to expand into the area. The problem is that the salt deposits would fill up the lagoons. More salt in the lagoons could be harmful to the whales and would probably kill the smaller fish the whales feed on.

The salt company intends to expand because the demand for salt is rising as the world's population rises. Nearly everyone needs a balanced amount of salt to stay healthy.

The Mexican government wants the salt company to expand in order to bring more jobs and money to the area. But the Mexican environmental agency and international groups are against the expansion because it could endanger the whales.

The world waits to see whether Mexico will choose pesos or whales, business or the environment. People need jobs and whales need lagoons. What would you do?

Turn the page.

Answer the questions below.

1 Tourists probably have the opinion that whale watching is

A more important than the salt industry.

B protected by the government.

C happening off all shorelines.

D an excellent reason to visit Mexico.

2 Which of the following best describes the main focus of the selection?

F facts about Pacific Gray whales

G conflict between business and nature

H sightseeing opportunities in Mexico

J things Mexico and Alaska have in common

3 Based on the selection, which of the following most likely approves of the salt company's expansion?

A the Mexican government

B the Mexican environmental agency

C international groups

D tourists

4 Based on the selection, does the author seem to think that the salt company's expansion is a good idea? Explain your answer.

_____

_____

_____

_____

5 Whales spend fewer than four months in Mexican waters. Why is the time they spend there so important to their survival?

_____

_____

_____

Name _____

Read the selection. Then answer the questions that follow.

The American Dream

In the early 1900s, few people dreamed they could ever own a car. Several small companies made "horseless carriages." Their prices were so high, very few people could afford them.

Henry Ford had his own dream. He wanted to build a car most people could afford. First, he had to design a car that cost a reasonable amount to build. He was so sure he could do it that in 1903, with about $28,000 (what many cars today cost), he started his own car company. It was named after him. More than one hundred years later, it is still making cars.

Henry Ford built cars people could afford by hiring many workers. Each one of them would do one task—like sewing the seat covers—for each car. This approach, called an assembly line, led to each worker being very fast and accurate. Within five years, Henry Ford's dream was on the road!

Turn the page.

Answer the questions below.

1 **Based on the first paragraph, which is an opinion people might have had in the early 1900s?**

A Someday I will be able to afford a car.

B There are many car makers to choose from.

C A car is called a horseless carriage.

D I don't think I'll ever own a car.

2 **Which of the following words from the second paragraph is a clue that Henry Ford had a strong opinion?**

F dream

G person

H $28,000

J company

3 **Based on the passage, which of the following appears to be a fact?**

A Henry Ford should have started making cars sooner.

B Henry Ford's cars were the best-made cars in the United States.

C People would have bought Henry Ford's cars at higher prices.

D The assembly line allowed Henry Ford to price cars reasonably.

4 **Explain the meaning of the last sentence.**

_____

_____

_____

_____

_____

_____

_____

_____

Name _____

Read the selection. Then answer the questions that follow.

Super Pets

Dogs come in all sizes. They can be as small as a loaf of bread or weigh more than an average fifth grader. Most dogs need daily walks and an area in which to run around. However, their owners feel they are well worth it.

Statistics show that the most popular pet dog in recent years is the Labrador retriever. Labs, as they are called, are generally playful and gentle and make excellent guide dogs for the visually impaired. They are also great partners for bird hunters because their strongest instinct is to fetch. Throw a ball in front of a Lab, and the dog will almost always run after it.

Purebred dogs are desirable in part because they usually have consistent traits. That is, if a breed is known for its energy and you want an energetic dog, you can get a dog of that breed and be pretty sure it will exercise with you. You will also have a good idea of how big a dog will get, which is useful information. If you like the way a particular breed looks, you can get a puppy knowing what the grown-up dog will look like.

If you are inclined to like mixed breed dogs, there are many to choose from in animal and rescue shelters. Mixed breed dogs often have the best traits of whatever breeds they include.

The best thing about any dog is that it will usually respond to love and care by loving its owner in return. That is probably why research has proven that petting a dog lowers stress levels.

Turn the page.

Answer the questions below.

1 **"Labrador retrievers are the most popular pet" is a statement of fact because**

  A Labs are gentle and playful.

  B statistics prove it.

  C Labs fetch by instinct.

  D most breeders choose to breed Labs.

2 **What phrase is a clue that the reader is reading a statement of fact?**

  F be pretty sure

  G have a good idea

  H if you are inclined

  J research has proven

3 **What is the main idea of the passage?**

  A Large dogs make better pets than small dogs.

  B Dogs are not worth the work it takes to care for them.

  C Picking out a dog involves a lot of research.

  D Purebreds are not better than mixed breeds.

4 **Which of the following is probably the reason pet owners have a favorable opinion of Labs?**

  F They are a purebred dog.

  G They help their owners reduce stress.

  H They have been the subject of research.

  J They like to work and play with people.

5 **Would petting a cat be likely to lower stress levels? Explain why or why not.**

_____

_____

_____

_____

_____

_____

_____

Read the selection. Then answer the questions that follow.

Hurricanes

Wind and water are two of the greatest forces in nature. When a force of spiraling wind forms over water, it is referred to as a hurricane. There is a season for hurricanes. In the Northern Hemisphere, hurricane season is from June to November. The hurricanes are named after both men and women using a somewhat confusing system.

When Europeans first came to America, no English, French, or Spanish was spoken here. The native inhabitants, or islanders, spoke Arawakan and called the tropical storm *hurakan*. The English word *hurricane* appeared around 1560.

Hurricanes are classified into five categories based on their wind speed. A Category One hurricane has winds of between 75 and 95 miles per hour. A Category Five hurricane has winds greater than 155 miles per hour. In more than one hundred years, only three Category Five hurricanes have hit the U.S. shoreline.

In the western Pacific area near China, a hurricane is referred to as a *typhoon* and in the Indian Ocean it is known as a *cyclone*. No matter what such a system is called, it carries with it the awesome power of nature.

Hurricanes differ from tornadoes in that hurricanes carry a massive amount of water, which adds greatly to their weight. How much does a hurricane weigh? A scientist found a way to measure this and found that a hurricane can weigh about 220 million tons. That is equivalent to the weight of 40 million elephants, more than have ever lived on Earth. As you can imagine, 40 million elephants moving at 75 miles per hour is quite a force to reckon with.

Turn the page.

Answer the questions below.

1 **What is the main idea of the passage?**

  A to persuade the reader to study hurricane warning systems

  B to inform the reader about the weight of an elephant

  C to help the reader imagine all the elephants that ever lived

  D to give the reader information about hurricanes and their weight

2 **Tom said, "The origin of the word *hurricane* is Spanish." Which paragraph contains the evidence that will prove whether this statement of fact is true or false?**

  F paragraph 2

  G paragraph 3

  H paragraph 4

  J paragraph 5

3 **The reference to 40 million elephants is used to support a statement of fact about—**

  A the categories of hurricanes.

  B the wind speed of hurricanes.

  C the seasons of hurricanes.

  D the weight of hurricanes.

4 **Based on the selection, give a statement of fact that explains a difference between a tornado and a hurricane.**

_____

_____

_____

_____

5 **Reread the last sentence of the first paragraph. Identify the statement of fact and the statement of opinion based on that sentence.**

_____

_____

_____

_____

Name _____

Read the selection. Then answer the questions that follow.

Helpful Hobbies

Jennifer and Trey were visiting their grandparents. Their grandmother knitted during the afternoon while their grandfather did woodworking in his "shop" in the garage.

When asked why she knitted, their grandmother smiled. "Knitting helps me think and relax. And I can make sweaters or blankets for you grandchildren. Want to try?"

With his grandmother knitting slowly to show him how, Trey tried. It was difficult and awkward. "In time, the motion will feel more natural," she told him. Trey was proud and surprised to see that the stitches make rows and that the rows added into what looked like the beginning of a scarf.

Jennifer wandered out to watch their grandfather work on a birdhouse. When asked why he spent so much time woodworking, he said, "My shop is a peaceful place, far from the busy world. Want to try?" Jennifer's grandfather put his hands over hers and showed her how to sand the rough surface. "Now, feel that. Doesn't that feel good?"

Jennifer smiled. "Feels like chocolate!"

Turn the page.

Answer the questions below.

1 **The author wants the reader to consider hobbies as**

A difficult.

B daring.

C fulfilling.

D boring.

2 **In the selection, the two hobbies are mainly presented as**

F different because one requires power tools.

G different because knitting produces something original.

H alike because both are peaceful and relaxing.

J alike because both produce items that can be used as gifts.

3 **The grandfather associates his hobby mostly with the**

A access to the outdoors it allows.

B usefulness of what he makes.

C place where he practices it.

D stages of a project.

4 **Jennifer's opinion is that the wood "feels like chocolate." On what fact about sanded wood is her opinion based?**

_____

_____

_____

_____

_____

_____

_____

_____

_____

_____

Name _____

Read the selection. Then answer the questions that follow.

Map Making: Where in the World Are You?

Throughout history, people have used different methods to locate themselves or places. People living in caves who wanted to return to a place or tell someone how to get there used drawings and symbols. The earliest map known was written on a clay tablet in 3000 B.C. In Egypt, in 1400 B.C., a map was drawn showing markers set along the Nile River. This helped to decide who paid how much in taxes. But when the Nile flooded, the markers washed away.

One famous map maker was Amerigo Vespucci, a trader, who signed his name to the maps he drew when he traveled to the New World. Many people thought *Amerigo* was the name of the new lands.

When Lewis and Clark explored the western United States, they used two poles connected by a thirty-three-foot long chain. Eighty chains measured half a mile. This was easier than pacing—measuring by counting footsteps—to determine distances. They also used the stars, sun, moon, and a compass.

Modern maps use symbols and a legend to indicate distances. For example, one inch on the United States map in an atlas usually equals 150 miles on land. One current method to measure distance involves the amount of time it takes a laser beam to reach from one point to a second point. Global Positioning Systems can bounce signals off satellites to measure a distance or find someone.

Turn the page.

Answer the questions below.

1 **What is the main idea of this selection?**

  A The reader will be involved in developing new methods of locating people and places.

  B Lewis and Clark's map-making methods were far better than methods used before.

  C Map-making has always been very important in the United States.

  D Ways of finding and recording the location of places have changed throughout history.

2 **The Egyptian maps using markers along the Nile were used mostly for**

  F vacation spots.

  G property boundaries.

  H tax calculations.

  J water level checks.

3 **Based on information in the selection, why did Lewis and Clark measure distance as they traveled?**

  A They had to make sure their map was correct.

  B No one had mapped the region they were exploring.

  C Measuring distance kept them from getting lost.

  D They were trying to go a certain number of miles.

4 **The selection is mostly made up of**

  F statements of opinion.

  G statements of fact.

  H some statements of opinion and some statements of fact.

  J very little fact but much opinion.

5 **Historically, map-making methods involved measurement of actual land. What does very modern map-making technology measure?**

_____

_____

_____

_____

_____

_____

Name _____

Read the selection. Then answer the questions that follow.

Video Game Thinking

Video games are very popular today but have been around for some time. The first game, invented in 1952, was a computer version of tick-tack-toe. Later, a tennis game and a space war game were created. Today, many people have or want a hand-held computer designed to play games.

Based on the popularity of electronic games, scientists took a closer look to see how the brain responds to them. In Japan, a scientist studied the levels of brain activity while study subjects were playing video games. He found that over a period of thirty minutes, less brain power was used for video games than for adding single numbers. He found that during computer games, the front part of the brain was not active. The front part of the brain is linked to controlling behavior. He claimed that playing computer games for too many hours would prevent young people from developing the part of the brain that controls behavior.

A U.S. scientist studied brain waves and found that video games improved the attention span of study subjects. The studied groups who played video games showed improvement in controlling their behavior and improvement in concentrating.

NASA plans to use video type games to help train pilots and astronauts to keep calm and pay attention.

Based on all the evidence so far, video games can be helpful or damaging, depending on what else you do with your time. Such games are no substitute for doing homework or reading.

Turn the page.

Answer the questions below.

1 **Which of the following ideas was not presented in the selection?**

   A Video games may not develop the whole brain.

   B Video games can improve concentration skills.

   C A half hour is how long you should play video games.

   D More and more video games have become available.

2 **Which is the main idea in the selection?**

   F The first video games were simple and not very popular.

   G Video games have been around for more than fifty years.

   H Hand-held computers are used by kids and adults.

   J Scientists have studied how video games affect the brain.

3 **What evidence would not prove that video games are popular?**

   A Five of your six best friends play video games.

   B Advertisements for video games appear on television.

   C Statistics show dramatic increases in video game sales.

   D One hundred percent of people surveyed have played a video game.

4 **What would be the most likely setting for a video game NASA would use?**

_____

_____

_____

_____

5 **What feature of computers that play only video games has probably contributed most to their popularity?**

_____

_____

_____

_____

Name _____

Read the selection. Then answer the questions that follow.

Hyde Park Teachers, Then and Now

Hyde Park Elementary likes balance. We want our students and our teachers to see that teaching is a job for both men and women. Back in 1990, more than twice as many of our teachers were women. Over the years, teachers have left to start their own families, retire, or move away. So we have hired new teachers. The number of men and women teachers at our school is by now almost equal. More important than whether a teacher is a man or a woman is whether a teacher cares about students and enjoys teaching. I am happy to say that we have set a good balance and increased the number of teachers. At the same time we have made sure we hire those we think are the very best for the job.

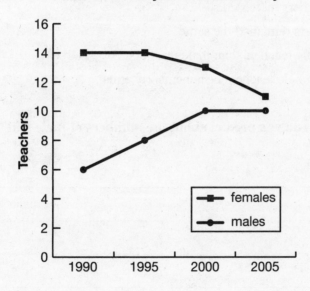

Teachers at Hyde Park Elementary

Turn the page.

Answer the questions below.

1 How many years are being compared on the line graph?

A five

B four

C sixteen

D 2005

2 The author wants readers to agree that Hyde Park Elementary has been hiring new teachers in a way that is

F careless.

G poor.

H exciting.

J fair.

3 Based on the line graph, which of the following did not happen between 2000 and 2005?

A The number of female teachers increased.

B The number of male teachers remained the same.

C There were still more female teachers than male teachers.

D The number of male and female teachers became nearly equal.

4 Based on the line graph, what do you predict about the numbers of male and female teachers in 2010?

_____

_____

_____

_____

_____

_____

_____

_____

5 Copyright © Pearson Education, Inc., or its affiliates. All Rights Reserved.

Name _____

Read the selection. Then answer the questions that follow.

Stewart's New Mascots

Congratulations, parents and students! Stewart Middle School's September outreach project to bring in a thousand dollars to donate to the Stewart Animal Shelter has been a big success. Students washed cars, sold T-shirts and bumper stickers, and made phone calls to neighbors and friends, asking for donations. In the competition among grades, the fifth graders won. This means that for all of October, groups of fifth graders will be going on a weekly field trip to the animal shelter to help out and pet the dogs and cats. The fifth graders will pick our mascots—one cat and one dog—who will appear on the ordered T-shirts. In November, groups of sixth graders will go on weekly field trips, and in December, groups of fourth graders will go.

Please ask your parents if they would like to volunteer to go with one or more groups. Those of you who want a puppy for Christmas might get to pick your gift out early!

If everything goes well at the animal shelter, we will plan another outreach project involving animals after the New Year. One project that has been suggested is "Team Clean-up." Small groups of students would go to Life Aquatic, a local pet store, and help with cleaning and caring for the fish and other animals. Learning to live with, respect, and care for animals is important. The Parents' Committee hopes you all agree and thanks you for your efforts.

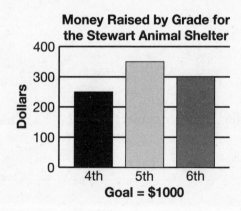

Money Raised by Grade for the Stewart Animal Shelter

Goal = $1000

Turn the page.

Answer the questions below.

1 The author wants readers to believe that fish and other aquatic animals are

A as deserving of care as any other creature.

B less likely to be attractive mascots.

C much more fun to help than shelter pets.

D harder to care for than dogs and cats.

2 Based on the text and the bar graph, why did the fifth graders most likely win?

F They sold the most T-shirts.

G They washed the most cars.

H They brought in the biggest donations.

J They agreed on mascots faster than the other grades.

3 Based on the text and the bar graph, why are the sixth graders going to the Animal Shelter before the fourth graders?

A Older students should go before younger ones.

B They brought in the second highest donations.

C The Parents' Committee voted that they would go next.

D The fourth graders will be working on the Life Aquatic project.

4 Based on the bar graph, how much did the sixth graders collect in donations?

F $1000

G $350

H $250

J $300

5 Will a graph like the one for the Animal Shelter project probably be made for the Life Aquatic Project? Explain your answer.

_____

_____

_____

_____

_____

_____

Name _____

Read the selection. Then answer the questions that follow.

Where We Spend Our Weekends

In a large study of Americans, it was found that the vast majority spend almost all their time indoors. During the week, of course, many people are at work, but there's no excuse for how many people spend the weekends missing out on the world—the world beyond our televisions and offices and cars and shopping malls. I wrote up my own survey and handed it out at my middle school to all the fifth graders. I am glad to report that I got back 100 percent of the surveys, even though I had to ask several people several times. My survey asked where students spent the majority of their weekend time, and I divided the categories of indoors and outdoors into time spent with friends or family. In the chart below, the *O* represents outdoors and the *I* represents indoors.

The good news is that a lot of fifth graders are spending most of their weekend time outdoors. (My survey was completed in April. The results might be different in, say, January, when it's cold and gets dark earlier. I will try to hand out another survey to the same students next year during winter so that the results can be directly compared.) However, many of them who spend their weekend time outdoors are with friends rather than with their families. I wondered if this was because adults are tired or have forgotten how to play, or if planning outdoor activities for the whole family seems like too much work.

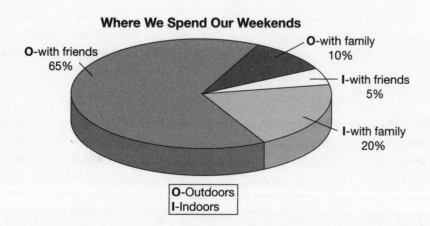

Where We Spend Our Weekends

O-with friends 65%
O-with family 10%
I-with friends 5%
I-with family 20%

O-Outdoors
I-Indoors

Turn the page.

Answer the questions below.

1 The author gives several possible reasons why children spend more outdoor time with their friends than with their families. Why do you think the author includes this information?

A to argue that they go out with their friends because their parents stay inside

B to show that children are healthier than adults because they go outside

C to warn children about growing up to be adults who forget how to have fun

D to explain why parents are too busy to spend time outdoors with them

2 Based on the selection and the pie graph, kids who are mostly indoors on the weekends are

F alone.

G reading.

H with friends.

J with family.

3 Based on the pie graph, what percentage of kids are mostly outdoors on the weekend?

A 75%

B 65%

C 10%

D 20%

4 Identify several places the author suggests people who are indoors on weekends spend their time.

_____

_____

_____

5 If the author subdivided the four general categories in the pie graph into specific activities (playing games, watching videos, doing yardwork, and so on), would the new pie graph show changes in the percentages in the four general categories shown now? Explain your answer.

_____

_____

_____

_____

Name _____

Read the selection. Then answer the questions that follow.

Saturday in Senegal

The club met every weekend in the travel aisle of the library.

"Whose turn?" Shanti whispered.

"Mine," Ryan whispered back, running his finger along the spines of the books. He grabbed one and sat down. Shanti sat next to him. They leaned against the wall of books. With the book propped between their laps, they studied the pictures. The Dakar market had tall, delicate arches of rough rock. The inside of each arch was paved with smooth white stones. Between each pair perched a sphere. The spheres were covered with multicolored tiles. Beyond the arches lay the Atlantic Ocean and the flat horizon.

They learned that Dakar is the capital of Senegal, a country in West Africa. The tiny country of Gambia stretched inland right into the middle of Senegal.

"Gambia is shaped like a tongue," Shanti said. "Next week, we're going to Gambia!"

Turn the page.

Answer the questions below.

1 **Why do Ryan and Shanti have their club meeting at the library each week?**

A to imagine visiting the places in travel books

B to do a report for their geography teacher

C to plan summer vacation trips for their families

D to study all the countries of West Africa

2 **Which of the following would make the *best* name for the club that Ryan and Shanti belong to?**

F Family Holidays Club

G The Book–Readers Club

H Library Helpers Club

J Imaginary Travelers Club

3 **Which of the following features of the setting is *most* important to the story?**

A A library is a place where all visitors are supposed to be quiet.

B A library holds way too many books for anybody ever to read.

C The tall library shelves make the aisle private like a clubhouse.

D The shelved books give the children something to lean against.

4 **What *mostly likely* happened at the club meeting last week? Explain why you think so, using information from the selection.**

_____

_____

_____

_____

_____

_____

_____

Name _____

Read the selection. Then answer the questions that follow.

Return of the Meerkat

I followed my nose into the kitchen. My older sister, Katy, was making fried chicken and potato salad because, she informed me, we were going on a Saturday picnic. Basically, she lured me into the car with food, and then she drove straight to Vandermeer Park. I did not want to go there ever again. It was the scene of my greatest humiliation. Only a month before, the Meerkats, our local softball team, had lost the end of the season game. I won't go into detail, but the loss had been my fault.

"You know," I said, angry at having been tricked, "there *are* other parks!"

"Now, Emmy," Katy said, pulling into the parking lot closest to the ball field. "You love this park. For years you've ridden your bike here, hung out with your friends, shot baskets, tossed balls. You made some fine base hits and home runs on that field. There's a lot more good than bad for you here."

I shuffled along beside her. I couldn't resist peering at the dugout and looking at the outfield. I couldn't help remembering. Freshly miserable, I trailed behind Katy to a shady patch of grass at least twenty yards from the field.

The chicken was fabulous, just spicy enough, and the potato salad had just the right amount of mayonnaise. I cast an eye over the entirety of the park, the swings, the merry-go-round, the tree I'd climbed most often. Stunned, I realized I was enjoying myself.

"OK," I said. "I love the park, no matter what embarrassing things I've done here."

Turn the page.

Answer the questions below.

1 **Which feature of the setting is *most* important to the plot?**

A the swings

B the picnic shelter

C the ballfield

D the parking lot

2 **Why does Katy take Emmy to Vandermeer Park?**

F to show her how much it has changed

G to climb a tree they both used to climb

H to discuss the last Meerkats ballgame

J to remind her how much she loves it

3 **Emmy says to her sister, "You know there *are* other parks!" What does Emmy mean by this statement?**

A Emmy is protesting a return to the site of her softball failure.

B Emmy has been spending most of her time at a better park.

C Emmy feels that she already spends too much time at Vandermeer.

D Emmy is making sure Katy knows about the other city parks.

4 **In the fourth paragraph, why does Emmy fall behind as she walks with Katy?**

F She pauses to see if any equipment is on the field.

G She is distracted by her memory of the game.

H She is angry at her sister and she wants to be alone.

J She turns around to go back to the car in the lot.

5 **What is Katy's plan on the day she takes Emmy to Vandermeer Park?**

_____

_____

_____

_____

_____

Name _____

Read the selection. Then answer the questions that follow.

Bobbie's Chance

Bobbie was a walking encyclopedia on baseball. She loved the sport like no other student in her school and examined everything she could uncover about it. She loved the crack of a wooden bat striking a ball into the distant left field. She loved the spectacle of field lights blazing into a warm summer night. She even loved the taste of dirt following a slide into home base. But Bobbie was in a serious predicament.

Overall, the only chance she ever got to play baseball was at annual family gatherings. Bobbie wasn't a very good player, but she believed that with a real coach she could really improve. Her dream was to play on the girl's baseball team at school. She was convinced that if she didn't communicate her desires, her entire life would remain the same forever. So she went to see Coach Annie Miller two days before tryouts. Last year she had not made the team, and she had not improved much since.

Bobbie crept toward the coach's office where she saw Coach Miller looking over some papers. She looked up, frowning, when Bobbie knocked on the open door.

Bobbie shuffled nervously to the desk and announced that she loved baseball and knew that with a lot of practice and effort she could improve. If Coach Miller would give her a chance, she knew she could contribute to the team. Coach Miller already knew Bobbie was not a naturally gifted athlete, but she saw fire in Bobbie's heart, and she knew that natural ability alone does not make a player great. She did give Bobbie a chance, and by the end of the season Bobbie won two awards: Most Improved Player and Best Team Spirit.

Turn the page.

Answer the questions below.

1 **What is the theme of the story?**

A Lacking a talent for what you love to do leads to suffering.

B Improvement through hard work is a sweet reward.

C Others often see talents in us that we cannot see ourselves.

D Hard work can lead anyone to succeed at sports.

2 **Based on the selection, which of the following conclusions about Coach Miller is probably not true?**

F She is interested in her players.

G She takes the team seriously.

H She tries to let all players spend some time playing in a real game.

J She regrets giving Bobbie a place on the team.

3 **Which of the following conclusions can you draw from the selection?**

A Bobbie would have found a way to play baseball even if Coach Miller hadn't given her a chance.

B Most of the girls didn't want Bobbie on the team.

C Bobbie was pleased with how her first season turned out.

D To be a champion, Bobbie spent all of her extra time playing baseball.

4 **What conclusions can you draw from the following statement? "Overall, the only chance she ever got to play baseball was at annual family gatherings."**

_____

_____

_____

5 **How do you think Bobbie would describe her life before she talked with Coach Miller?**

_____

_____

_____

Name _____

Read the selection. Then answer the questions that follow.

Hueco Tanks State Historical Park

Have you ever seen very old paintings on rock walls? Hueco Tanks State Historical Park, about thirty miles east of El Paso, Texas, is home to some of the best Native American rock art in the country. The park's three huge rock hills are covered with nearly five thousand paintings of things people did in their daily lives.

Hueco is a Spanish word that means "hollow." The area is called Hueco Tanks because there are deep pits in the rocks. The pits collected rainwater. The Native Americans who lived there could almost always depend on these "tanks" to hold the water they needed.

Scientists have studied many pieces of pottery and tools that were found in this area. They believe that humans started living here ten thousand years ago.

Turn the page.

Answer the questions below.

1 If you were a Native American living at Hueco Tanks two thousand years ago, you would

A usually have to search for water.

B have water sometimes.

C usually have water.

D run out of water often.

2 If you were trying to identify the location where the ancient Native Americans of Hueco Tanks had once lived, you would look for

F rainwater.

G a herd of buffalo.

H a desert.

J paintings on rocks.

3 Based on information in the first paragraph, the Hueco Tanks rock art would most likely include pictures of

A people preparing their meals.

B special occasions only.

C men driving farm equipment.

D unusual historical events.

4 Based on the selection, what objects were left by the Native Americans of Hueco Tanks, and what do these objects suggest about how they lived?

_____

_____

_____

_____

_____

_____

_____

_____

Name _____

Read the selection. Then answer the questions that follow.

The African Elephant Family

Did you know that elephants have very strong family units? Elephant families work, play, eat, sleep, and travel together. The oldest and most experienced female elephant, called a cow, is always in charge of her family. She is the matriarch, meaning she directs the family in everything they do.

Her family usually consists of her daughters and her grandchildren. She may even take charge of a younger sister and her children. A typical African elephant family has six to twelve members. However, it is not uncommon in some areas to have more elephants in a single-family unit.

As the male, or bull, children mature, they begin to exercise their independence from their family. They usually begin by spending bits of time outside of the group, and eventually leave the family to join other males in a band of bulls.

Of the female family groups and bull bands, the female groups appear to maintain a stronger social connection. Even if a female group splits into related groups, they will probably continue to travel together as they migrate from place to place in search of food. Some people call these related groups "bond groups." Several bond groups together form a clan.

It is normal for female family groups to split, forming two family groups. Generally, a group will split over disagreements in the family or because the available food supply is too low for a large group. When they experience food shortages, family units will typically split so that finding sufficient food will be easier for both groups.

When a matriarch dies, her eldest daughter will most likely take charge of the family.

Turn the page.

Answer the questions below.

1 Which of the following describes the *male* members of a typical African Elephant family group?

A The males are young, immature children.

B The males are the ones who search for food.

C The males are the leaders of the family.

D The males are afraid of the female leader.

2 What can you not generalize from the elephant family to the human family?

F Both have a strong family bond.

G Both provide social connections.

H Males generally form their own group.

J Groups tend to develop into smaller groups.

3 Based on the selection, which of the following is probably true?

A Sister cows are never in the same group.

B Some bulls stay with their original family.

C Younger cows stay with their matriarch.

D Bull bands never interact with female family groups.

4 Based on the selection, which of the following groups would be most unusual?

F a female family of three

G a female family with only two cows

H a bull band of two bulls

J a female family joining a band of bulls

5 In general, how do you think African elephant families and human families are alike?

_____

_____

_____

_____

_____

_____

Name _____

Read the selection. Then answer the questions that follow.

Humpback Whales

Instead of teeth, the humpback whale has baleen plates inside its mouth. Baleen plates contain stiff, comb-like structures that are somewhat like a stiff paintbrush. After the humpback takes in a big gulp of seawater, the baleen holds food in and lets the water flow back out. Humpbacks are larger than toothed whales and have two blowholes in their heads.

These amazing mammals can dive to five hundred feet under the ocean's surface, but can stay under for only thirty minutes at a time. As humpbacks descend, water pressure compresses the air in their lungs. The oxygen is then sent to their brains and hearts. This keeps them alert and healthy under the water. Only when they rise to the surface can the whales breathe again.

The humpbacks gulp huge quantities of seawater, catching krill (tiny shrimplike animals), mackerel, herring, and other sea animals in their baleen. Occasionally, they may perform a specific group action to assemble their food. They use their powerful flat tail, called a fluke, to swim quickly in a circle as they release air bubbles. The bubbles corral the sea animals into a cluster. The whales continue to swim in a tighter and tighter circle, containing all the fish until they are ready to whirl through the circle with their mouths open. Each whale devours about one ton of food every day.

Humpbacks are verbal animals, able to make different kinds of sounds, such as whistles, squeals, and moans. Whistling and singing are the ways they "talk" to each other.

Today there are only about 400,000 humpback whales in the world, making them an endangered species.

Turn the page.

Answer the questions below.

1 **Which of the following would humpback whales probably never do?**

A chew up krill

B swim in a circle

C dive to five hundred feet

D eat with other whales

2 **Based on how humpback whales eat, what portion of food in a gulp of seawater is probably eaten?**

F all

G some

H most

J none

3 **What probably happens to a whale after thirty minutes under water?**

A Its oxygen begins to run low.

B It swims in a tighter circle.

C Its blowholes must be cleared.

D It has finished eating its meal.

4 **Based on the selection, what are the chances that two humpbacks who had never encountered each other before would be able to communicate? Explain your answer.**

_____

_____

_____

_____

5 **The author states that humpbacks can stay underwater for only thirty minutes. What generalization can be made based on the clue word "only"?**

_____

_____

_____

Name _____

Read the selection. Then answer the questions that follow.

The Geometry of a Shoe

Many of the simple items we use daily are, in fact, mysteries to us. Take, for example, our shoes. They have a basic purpose—to protect our feet. We hardly consider their usefulness. We think about whether the pair we're wearing suits our mood. Shoe designers are the only ones who understand the geometry of a shoe. Regular folks know a shoe has a heel and a sole, but that's about it.

Once you understand the beauty of a shoe's construction, you may never look at one in quite the same, careless way you used to. You'll notice if a vamp is plain or fancy, and maybe even whether there's a seam along the counter. You'll be grateful that your sneakers do not have a steel shank . . . and that your winter boots do.

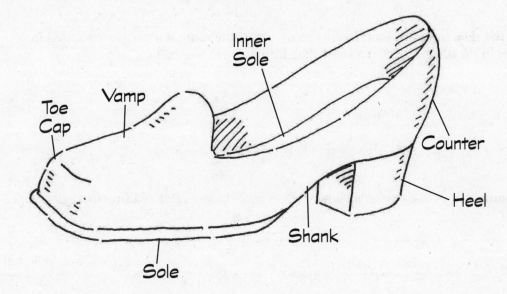

Turn the page.

Answer the questions below.

1 If a shoe had a steel shank, it would *probably*

   A be a lighter shoe with a thinner, higher heel.

   B have an all-leather vamp.

   C be a stronger shoe that does not bend as much.

   D have a seam on the counter.

2 If a designer wanted to turn the shoe in the diagram into one that laced up, which part of the shoe would change *most*?

   F counter

   G vamp

   H heel

   J sole

3 Which part of the shoe would be *most likely* to stay about the same if a designer wanted to change the shoe in the diagram from a solid shoe into an open sandal?

   A heel

   B inner sole

   C counter

   D toe cap

4 How does the author hope the reader's view of shoes will change after reading this selection?

_____

_____

_____

_____

_____

_____

_____

_____

_____

Name _____

Read the selection. Then answer the questions that follow.

Building a Bat House

There are many reasons you should build a bat house. One reason is that bats are a natural predator of the mosquito, a pest most of us do not want in our yards. A second reason is that bats are a valuable natural resource and should be protected. It takes little time to make a fine shelter for a colony of bats, and you'll be doing your part to help a species survive.

Follow the instructions below to build a bat house that will attract bats:

1. Gather the tools and materials.

2. Measure and cut cedar into three pieces: $26\frac{1}{2}$" x 24", $16\frac{1}{2}$" x 24", and 5" x 24". Long and wide bat houses built from cedar (rough on the inside) are best, though you can use exterior plywood $\frac{1}{2}$" thick or thicker.

3. Measure and cut a strip of wood 1" x 2" x 13", and two strips of wood 1" x 2" x $14\frac{1}{2}$". Attach these together (see illustration A).

4. Attach strong plastic mesh ($\frac{1}{2}$" squares) inside the front and back pieces.

5. Use galvanized screws to assemble the house to keep the house strong.

6. Caulk all seams to help keep the interior dry and warm.

7. Never paint the inside of a bat house, and use exterior paint on the outside. Use the chart at the right to select the best color.

COLOR	AVERAGE SUMMER TEMPERATURE
Black	Less than 85°F
Dark brown or dark gray	85°F to 95°F
Medium brown or medium gray	95°F to 100°F
White or light colors	More than 100°F

8. Mount the bat house facing south and at least fifteen feet above the ground on either a pole, garage, barn, or your house; avoid trees, and remove anything, such as tree limbs or leaves, that could prevent the bats from entering their new residence.

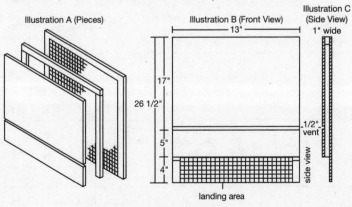

Illustration A (Pieces)   Illustration B (Front View)   Illustration C (Side View)

Turn the page.

Answer the questions below.

1 The front view illustration shows a $\frac{1}{2}$" vent. Why might a vent be necessary in a bat house?

  A to allow food and water to be put inside

  B to allow the air to flow freely

  C to prevent other animals from entering the house

  D to provide a way for small bats to escape

2 Why do you think mesh is attached to the inside walls of the house (Step 4)?

  F to make the inside look good

  G to hold the pieces of the house together

  H to keep the temperature steady

  J to give the bats something to hold on to

3 Why do you think the author *most likely* included the first paragraph?

  A to persuade everyone to protest the growing loss of forests

  B to argue that a bat house is good for both bats and people

  C to explain why bats have a hard time finding a place to live

  D to entertain with an image of a bat chasing down a mosquito

4 As shown in illustration B, the inside of the bat house is only one inch thick. Why would the house be so narrow?

  F Bats cannot sleep in narrow spaces.

  G Bats are comfortable in narrow spaces.

  H The designer preferred a thin house.

  J The house is designed for only two bats.

5 Based on the information in the chart, why might white not be a good color to choose for a bat house?

_____

_____

_____

_____

_____

_____

Name _____

Read the selection. Then answer the questions that follow.

Feng Shuí and You

Today many people around the world practice a very old Chinese belief system. They believe that everything in nature has an energy called Chi (chee), and there is positive Chi and negative Chi. The way we use Chi determines the outcome of everything we do. This is called Feng Shuí (fung SHWAY).

As a young person who is constantly growing, exploring, and changing, you might find Feng Shuí useful as you create your own environment. Let's look at your bedroom.

You spend about a third of your life in this space. Because your early years are formative (that is, you are being formed), it is important that your bedroom reflect your personality. This will help you stay comfortable as you grow and reach for your true potential.

The tool you'll use when deciding where to place the furniture in your room is called a ba-gua (ba GUA). Follow these steps:

Step 1: Draw a floor plan of your room. Include the windows, doors, and furniture.

Step 2: Draw four angled lines across the floor plan to make eight triangular sections.

Step 3: Use a compass to locate North. Mark it on your floor plan. Next, locate South, East, and West and mark them on your floor plan. Then add Northeast, Southeast, Southwest, and Northwest.

Step 4: Study the ba-gua below. You may want to move your furniture to the sections that will improve your activities in those areas. For example, if you and a family member seem to disagree a lot, you might want to put a blooming plant in the Southwest section of your room to create harmony.

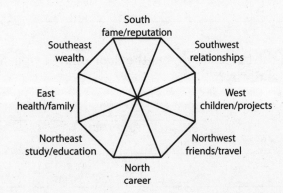

Turn the page.

Answer the questions below.

1 What does the author *most likely* want you to do after reading the selection?

   A learn to use a compass

   B get some new blooming plants

   C clean up your bedroom

   D plan where to put furniture

2 If you wanted to improve your study habits, what would you put in the Northeast section of your room?

   F a bed

   G some plants

   H a dresser

   J a desk

3 If you had a disagreement with your little brother or sister, in what area of your room would you want to make sure your Chi was positive?

   A South

   B Southwest

   C West

   D Northwest

4 If your dream was to travel to other countries and make new friends there, how might you use Feng Shuí to keep you mindful of your goal?

_____

_____

_____

_____

5 If you used the ba-gua to design the floor plan of your house, where would you want to put the family den and why?

_____

_____

_____

_____

Name _____

Read the selection. Then answer the questions that follow.

Hot Air Balloons

Every year hundreds of thousands of people around the world delight in riding in hot air balloons. However, floating through the air is not a fresh idea. People studied ways to lift things from the ground two thousand years ago.

Many inventors, fascinated by hot air balloons, designed modern flying machines. But it wasn't until the 1960s that taking a ride in a hot air balloon became popular. This new adventure ride started with Ed Yost, who designed, built, and sold his balloons as sporting goods.

Because interest in ballooning has remained very strong, people like Ed continue to improve the balloons. As a rule, modern balloons have unusual shapes, are colorful, and come with special safety gear. This wonderful yet simple method of travel captures the imagination of everyone, young and old alike.

Turn the page.

Answer the questions below.

1 Which generalization can you best make from the facts in this selection?

  A Balloons were not used for fun until Ed Yost made his balloon.

  B If Ed Yost hadn't made his balloon, we wouldn't have colorful balloons today.

  C Most scientists like hot air balloons.

  D Balloons have changed greatly over the years.

2 What conclusion can you draw about the author's view of hot air balloons?

  F They are a growing business.

  G They are an old practice.

  H They are a costly hobby.

  J They are a slow way to travel.

3 Which of the following statements about Ed Yost is not a generalization?

  A He helped shape public interest in ballooning today.

  B He probably made a lot of money making hot air balloons.

  C He studied the balloons the people before him made.

  D He made colorful hot air balloons.

4 The last sentence states, "This wonderful yet simple method of travel captures the imagination of everyone, young and old alike." Explain why this is a faulty generalization.

_____

_____

_____

_____

_____

_____

_____

_____

Name _____

Read the selection. Then answer the questions that follow.

Taking a Chance

When Joseph handed Ms. Taylor his assignment, he couldn't have imagined how writing a short story would lead to more than a grade.

Joseph, who was shy, had few close friends. In his art class, students usually discussed modern painters and techniques for mixing paint. He kept quiet. No one except Karen seemed to notice him at all.

Joseph wanted to invite Karen to see the Jackson Pollock painting exhibit at the local museum. Every time he had an opportunity to bring it up, he'd start by talking about his own painting. He knew his work was not nearly as good as Karen's—she was a natural—but he wasn't sure where else to begin. He never got to the invitation before the bell rang.

When Joseph received an A+ on his story about a boy trying to ask a girl to an art opening, he was amazed. He knew that writing was fun and came easily to him, but he didn't realize he was good at it. Ms. Taylor's comments made him think he had a special talent, kind of like Karen's for painting. Ms. Taylor encouraged him to enter an upcoming national writing contest.

Initially, Joseph didn't want to enter the contest. He was worried about losing his new pride in himself if he didn't win. But Ms. Taylor insisted that taking risks was part of knowing who you are and what you can do.

Joseph finally agreed to submit his story to the contest. When he won second place, he was still proud of himself—of his writing and of his daring to enter the contest. He felt so good he took the risk of asking Karen to a movie, and she said yes.

Turn the page.

Answer the questions below.

1 What generalization can you make about Joseph and Karen's friendship?

A Friends talk about specific topics.

B Friends inspire you to do your best.

C Not all conversations between friends are easy.

D The best friends have different talents.

2 Joseph learned he had a special talent. What generalization can you make about finding your own talent?

F Someone else may have to point out your talent for you to see it.

G Once you know what you're talented at, your whole life changes.

H Everyone has a talent for something.

J Girls are usually better than boys at painting.

3 Ms. Taylor told Joseph that there are good reasons to take risks. Which of the following is probably not a good reason?

A To impress someone specific

B To learn how much you are capable of

C To feel good about having tried

D To face the fear of defeat

4 What conclusion can you draw about how the contest may have influenced Joseph's artistic efforts?

F He will worry that the good story was a fluke.

G He will try harder to be a better painter.

H Stories based on real life will be his focus.

J Writing will interest him more than painting.

5 Joseph's behavior changed after he won second place in the contest. Based on that change, what generalization can you apply to your life?

_____

_____

_____

_____

_____

Read the selection. Then answer the questions that follow.

By the Light of the Moons

Menzat was an ordinary Sutpori kid in the pod where he lived on the planet of Konkul. He ate great sandwiches for lunch, participated in regular family activities, and had several friends his age. Life was generally peaceful where he lived. He wondered whether things outside the Sutpori Wall, where the Siserem people lived, were the same or different.

Menzat had heard stories about the Siserems and a special ability they had. They were a yellowish color by day, and at night, when the moons were full, Siserems glowed. Menzat and others on his pod were mainly a dark blue and most had bulky knots between their eyebrows. They were too dark to glow in the light of the moons. Menzat himself felt a little envious of the Siserems. Glowing the way they did, they were probably dazzling.

Late one night, a thunderous crash outside Menzat's bedroom window startled him. Peering out, he saw a glowing Siserem, about his own age, who had just scaled the Sutpori Wall. Menzat whispered a loud hello and asked him what he was doing. The Siserem said his name was Rubian. He said he had decided to climb the wall to see if what everyone said was true—that the Sutpori were shining blue like polished stone.

Menzat climbed down the tree outside his window. It was a cloudy night, so it was darker than usual. "Because you're glowing, you'll be able to see," he said. In the light of Rubian's glowing skin, Menzat held out his hand. Rubian reached out and shook it. They both laughed.

Turn the page.

Answer the questions below.

1 Based on the story, a pod is probably like a

   A house.

   B gym.

   C library.

   D fortress.

2 Based on Menzat's attitude toward the Siserem, he views people different from him with

   F fear.

   G envy.

   H curiosity.

   J expectation.

3 Based on the story, what can you say about Menzat and Rubian?

   A Their daily lives are similar.

   B They are the same age and size.

   C Each wants to know about the other.

   D Both stay up very late every night.

4 Based on the story, who is more bold and daring, Menzat or Rubian? Explain why.

_____

_____

_____

_____

5 What happened during the meeting between Menzat and Rubian that suggests they liked each other?

_____

_____

_____

_____

Read the selection. Then answer the questions that follow.

Letter to My Granddaughter

Dear Rennie,

Your life is different from mine at your age. The fifth grade for me was a time for exploration and self-discovery. Generally, you have a better idea of who you are and what you want. Take your clothes, for example. You won't listen to salesclerks who try to convince you to purchase something you detest. Your self-confidence will always help you accomplish what you want.

You're a good kid with good friends. All together, you make up a mighty force that governments, businesses, and schools take very seriously. You are and will always be a powerful group.

You're on the right path, Rennie. Don't forget it. But if you do, I'll always be nearby to remind you of the things you do best.

Love,

Nanna

Turn the page.

Answer the questions below.

1 **From the tone of this letter, you know that**

A Rennie makes Nanna worried.

B Nanna is far away.

C Rennie has many friends.

D Nanna is proud of Rennie.

2 **What does Nanna mean when she states that Rennie and her friends are "a powerful group"?**

F Rennie and her friends are already important to society.

G Rennie and her friends will control government, business, and education.

H Rennie and her friends can get what they want right now if they demand it.

J Rennie and her friends will all want to be in charge at work someday.

3 **With which of the following generalizations would Nanna most likely agree?**

A Most girls today are more confident than girls were fifty years ago.

B Fifth grade has always been a time for exploration and self-discovery.

C Overall, even confident people appreciate compliments.

D Most fifth graders have a clear idea of who they are.

4 **How did Nanna feel about herself when she was in the fifth grade?**

_____

_____

_____

_____

Name _____

Read the selection. Then answer the questions that follow.

Iceberg C-19

NASA radar equipment deep in space records amazing things on Earth that help scientists understand what is happening. One event that caught their attention was something that happened in Antarctica in May 2002. An iceberg calved off, or broke away from, the western face of the Ross Ice Shelf. Although the calving of icebergs happens often without harming the environment, the calving of this iceberg, called C-19, had a different result.

Scientists grew concerned when C-19 splashed into the Ross Sea because it was almost twice the size of Rhode Island. Even though Rhode Island is the smallest state in the United States, an iceberg that size, let alone one twice that size, is enormous.

When C-19 fell into the Ross Sea, it covered up an important food source for all the local marine life. Phytoplankton (FY toh PLANK tun), tiny free-floating plants that live in the water, depend on sunbeams in order to grow. It was impossible for sunbeams to reach the phytoplankton in the water underneath with C-19, a huge mass, floating in the water above them. Therefore, the growth of new plant matter was reduced by more than 90 percent. Because phytoplankton are at the bottom of the food chain, every animal above them depends on them for life. If there are no phytoplankton for the next level above of marine animals to eat, those animals and the animals higher up in the food chain are in great danger.

Having studied for many years what happens when icebergs calve, scientists generally now believe that the numbers of marine plants and animals will drop in areas where icebergs exist.

Turn the page.

Answer the questions below.

1 Why do you think the author chose to compare the size of C-19 to the size of Rhode Island?

A to test the reader's knowledge of the size of U.S. states

B to give the reader an idea of the iceberg's size

C to imply that C-19 was smaller than other states

D to show that C-19 was not important

2 The phrase *marine life* in paragraph three means

F all plants that live in the sea.

G all animals that live in the sea.

H all phytoplankton.

J all plants and animals that live in the sea.

3 Which generalization can you make from the selection?

A All icebergs will calve in time.

B Icebergs keep sunlight away from all phytoplankton.

C Calved icebergs in Antarctica will always be large.

D Scientists never know what to expect when an iceberg calves.

4 Which of the following conclusions cannot be drawn based on the selection?

F Marine life depend on phytoplankton.

G Icebergs calved off can cause problems for the environment.

H Sunlight is important to underwater plant life too.

J NASA has underwater radar equipment.

5 What other important information might space radar equipment reveal to scientists?

_____

_____

_____

_____

_____

_____

Name _____

Read the selection. Then answer the questions that follow.

Dinosaur Dreams

In the movie *Jurassic Park*, a mad scientist created dinosaurs after they had been gone for millions of years. He used dinosaur DNA, a blood component that he found in the fluids of a mosquito. That insect was found inside an orange stone. Is it possible to bring dinosaurs back to life today? Even though many people are fascinated by the creatures, the answer is no.

There are ways to save DNA, but it breaks down over time even when it's protected. So over millions of years, much of DNA is lost. The sample is then useless. Also, even if we could remove the dinosaur blood from a mosquito inside a stone, we would still have a problem. It would be impossible to separate the dinosaur's DNA from the mosquito's DNA.

But let's make believe that we could find pure dinosaur DNA. We would then have to put it into an egg of the exact same type of dinosaur. Only then could the baby dinosaur develop. This too is an impossible task.

Let's make believe some more. Let's make believe that we could find the right egg, put the DNA in it, and hatch it. Now we have a baby dinosaur. How would we keep it alive? Our world is nothing like it was 65 million years ago. There are so many germs for which the baby dinosaur would have no natural defense. Plus, the food that dinosaurs ate no longer exists.

It's interesting to think about dinosaurs living in today's world. However, it is not likely to happen.

Turn the page.

Answer the questions below.

1 DNA breaks down over time even if it is protected. What conclusion can you draw from this statement?

A DNA cannot be used before it breaks down.

B DNA starts breaking down immediately.

C It takes millions of years for DNA to break down.

D We have not yet found a way to keep DNA from breaking down.

2 Which of the following is true of germs?

F There were no germs in the time of dinosaurs.

G Germs today are more dangerous than they used to be.

H Animals are resistant only to the germs of their time.

J There are more germs now than when dinosaurs lived.

3 What can you generalize about the popularity of the movie *Jurassic Park?*

A People do not demand scientific accuracy in movies.

B *Jurassic Park* was popular only because it was science fiction.

C Most people are fascinated by dinosaurs.

D Dinosaurs were killed by modern germs.

4 If a dinosaur were hatched today, it would not be able to survive. From this fact, what conclusions can you draw about the changes that have occurred on Earth?

_____

_____

_____

_____

5 What can you conclude about the author's interests and background based on the language and tone of this selection?

_____

_____

_____

Read the selection. Then answer the questions that follow.

Sasha Plants a Vegetable Garden

Sasha wanted to plant a vegetable garden in her yard. However, she shared the yard with her neighbor Elaine, and Sasha knew that Elaine would not be pleased to see her digging around. Elaine did not like changes of any kind, and she would be likely to complain. So, Sasha devised a plan to persuade Elaine to let her plant the garden.

Sasha invited Elaine over for lunch, serving soup and a salad. When Elaine said how much she liked the soup, Sasha said, "I made it from potatoes that Simon is growing in his garden." When Elaine said how tasty the salad was, Sasha replied, "I made it from spinach from Grace's garden."

"Hmmm," said Elaine. "Maybe we should plant some vegetables. Then we could eat fresh food all the time."

"Great idea," said Sasha smiling to herself. "We can buy seeds tomorrow."

Turn the page.

Answer the questions below.

1 **Which of the following best describes Sasha's character?**

   A She loves flowers.

   B She is thoughtful.

   C She likes to cook.

   D She is not a good listener.

2 **Why did Elaine decide to plant a garden?**

   F Sasha told Elaine that they can sell the vegetables.

   G Elaine read an article in a magazine about gardening.

   H Sasha and Elaine visited their friends Grace and Simon.

   J Elaine ate fresh food from other people's gardens.

3 **Which of the following best describes the conflict in the story?**

   A Sasha wants to plant a garden, but she knows Elaine will not want to.

   B Elaine wants to build a fence, but she knows Sasha will not agree.

   C Simon wants to grow carrots, but Sasha wants to grow spinach and lettuce.

   D Grace wants to have lunch with Elaine, but Elaine is too busy gardening.

4 **What is the author *most likely* trying to persuade readers of this story to do?**

Read the selection. Then answer the questions that follow.

A Wrinkle Just in Time

Everyone who knows me knows that I love science fiction and the fantastic things described in it. But recently when my brother, who's six, asked me to make up a story, I discovered that my imagination was mired in the real world.

My parents had gone out, leaving us with Tee-Cee. We love Tee-Cee. She charms us with compliments and grandmotherly affection until about nine o'clock, and then she falls asleep in my dad's recliner. Sometimes she snores. I usually read Bobbin (my brother Bobby) a bedtime story, tuck him in, and put myself to bed with my own book. But Bobbin didn't want me to read a story that night.

"Make one up, Julie," he demanded. "Make it weird, like the stories *you* like to read." But all I could think of were real stories, problems that could happen between friends, things that might happen at school. My imagination was trapped in the real world. I thought of Cinderella and all the old fairytales he'd probably already heard.

"All I can think of is real life or fairytales," I had to tell him. "Real life is pretty boring. The other stuff you've heard."

"You can make something up," he said. "Start it, 'A girl and her little brother wake up and look out the window, and their house is on Mars.'"

"Okay," I said. I struggled to see our house on a barren planet. (You can't afford to fail in front of a little brother.) "The land is gray and the sky is pink." Suddenly, my imagination yawned like a waking cat. "And there are no other houses, or buildings, or people, or trees."

"It's gonna be a scary one!" Bobbin chirped gleefully, sliding deeper under the covers.

Turn the page.

Answer the questions below.

1 **What is the climax of this selection?**

   A The speaker fails in front of her little brother.

   B Bobbin asks to hear a made-up bedtime story.

   C The speaker's imagination starts to work again.

   D The babysitter falls asleep right at nine o'clock.

2 **Why did Bobbin ask for a "weird" story?**

   F He likes science fiction stories.

   G Those are the kind his big sister reads.

   H He thinks that real life is boring.

   J Those are the kind Tee-Cee tells him.

3 **Why does Julie try to get out of telling Bobbin a story?**

   A She thinks Tee-Cee should be telling him a story.

   B She believes the stories she knows are boring.

   C She wants to go to bed and read her own book.

   D She is tired of telling the same story over and over.

4 **How does the start of Julie's story make Bobbin respond?**

   F with excitement

   G in a restless way

   H with fear

   J in a sleepy way

5 **What is the author _most likely_ trying to persuade readers to believe about their imaginations?**

_____

_____

_____

_____

_____

_____

Name _____

Read the selection. Then answer the questions that follow.

Back in the World

My brother makes big airy pronouncements. "See it, be it," he says. His advice, in fact, is mostly air. But I wanted, desperately, to run faster. Michael advised me to imagine myself crossing the finish line at a precise time, a little faster than my times in my last three races, in the Saturday Turkey Trot.

By Friday, I could hardly talk because I was too busy holding onto an image of myself crossing that line in 28 minutes, 45 seconds. It had to be under 29 minutes.

"Sweetheart?" my mother said. "Your grandmother's been here two hours and you've hardly talked to her."

"The race," I explained. "'See it, be it.' I'm very busy seeing it."

"Well, what I see is you being rude to your grandmother."

Guess where Michael's big airy pronouncements originated?

My grandmother Janie Mae is more fun, she remarks, than a barrel of monkeys. I occasionally wish I could compare the two firsthand, but no one will give me permission to have even one monkey, never mind a barrel. "I'm sorry I haven't talked to you yet," I said contritely, sitting on the arm of the sofa and leaning over to hug her. "Michael advised me to imagine running the race tomorrow in a specific time, and that's all I can think about."

She rolled her eyes and said, "That's his individual opinion. Mine is to quit thinking and just feel everything. Running's supposed to be *fun*, isn't it?"

As I ran, I couldn't hold the image of the time clock reading 28:45. I began to see instead—trees and other runners and the sky—and I felt . . . *happy*! And I felt that way for almost the whole 28 minutes and 52 seconds!

Turn the page.

Answer the questions below.

1 **What is the main conflict in the story?**

  A The speaker's brother and grandmother disagree.

  B The speaker's parents refuse to purchase a monkey.

  C The speaker seeks a plan to run faster in the next race.

  D The speaker's mother thinks the speaker is being rude.

2 **The speaker thinks Michael's advice is usually**

  F silly.

  G wise.

  H mean.

  J useful.

3 **The reader understands that, at the start of the race, the speaker was planning**

  A to quit running if she ran the race in over 29 minutes.

  B to follow Michael's advice and hold her time in mind.

  C to accept a race time that was likely to exceed 29 minutes.

  D to follow her grandmother's advice and just enjoy running.

4 **The speaker's grandmother talked with her before the race. How do you think the speaker would have felt during the race if that conversation had *not* taken place? Explain your answer.**

_____

_____

_____

_____

5 **How is the author trying to persuade us to feel about the goals we may set for ourselves?**

_____

_____

_____

_____

Name _____

Read the selection. Then answer the questions that follow.

How to Learn to Cook

Being able to cook is an important skill. Some people find it challenging to cook, but cooking becomes easier the more you do it. When you are first learning to cook, you can follow a recipe, which will tell you exactly what to do. For example, below is a recipe for making mashed potatoes. By following recipes like this one, you can learn to cook anything!

Mashed Potatoes
2 pounds of baking potatoes, peeled
3 tablespoons of butter
3/4 cup of milk
Salt and pepper
Boil the potatoes in a pot of salted water for about 30 minutes. When the potatoes are soft, drain the water and mash the potatoes, using a fork or a wooden spoon. Return the mashed potatoes to the pot, and over low heat add the butter and milk while stirring.
Add salt and pepper for flavor.

Turn the page.

Answer the questions below.

1 How many tablespoons of butter does the recipe call for?

   A one

   B two

   C three

   D four

2 Which of the following actions is not mentioned in the recipe?

   F boiling

   G draining

   H mashing

   J serving

3 Which of the following best states the main idea of the selection?

   A You can learn to cook by following recipes.

   B Mashed potatoes take a long time to make.

   C Most people never learn how to cook for themselves.

   D Collecting recipes will make you a better cook.

4 Why do you think the author included the recipe for mashed potatoes in this selection?

_____

_____

_____

_____

_____

_____

_____

_____

_____

_____

Read the selection. Then answer the questions that follow.

How to Order from a Menu

Almost every restaurant in the United States has a menu that lists the food items you can order. A menu also shows how much each dish or item costs and may be organized by category. For example, many menus list appetizers, salads, main courses, and desserts separately.

Some menus, such as those you find in Chinese restaurants, also list main courses by the type of ingredient. You might see listings for pork dishes, beef dishes, and vegetarian dishes for people who do not eat meat. Restaurants provide menus so that you know exactly what you can order. Below is a menu from a pizza restaurant.

When you order from a menu such as this one, you can first look over all the items and then decide what you would like to eat. You should also consider the range of prices listed and how many people will be eating. For example, when you order a pizza, you may want to order a small pizza for one or two people and a large pizza for a group of four or more.

Jill's Pizza

Pizza Type	Small	Medium	Large
Cheese	$8.00	$11.00	$13.00
Pepperoni	$10.00	$13.00	$15.00
Vegetarian	$13.50	$16.50	$18.50
Super Special*	$14.50	$17.50	$19.50

Add your own toppings. The following toppings are available: anchovies, artichokes, olives, bacon, bleu cheese, chicken, garlic, goat cheese, green peppers, sausage, jalapeño peppers, mushrooms, onions, pepperoni, pesto, pineapple, salami, tomatoes, zucchini.

Salads

Green salad $2.50   Tomato salad $3.50

Beverages

Soda $1.00   Milk $1.00   Bottled Water $1.00

*The Super Special pizza includes sausage, peppers, olives, garlic, and extra cheese.

Delivery from 5:00 P.M. to midnight every day.

Turn the page.

Answer the questions below.

1 Which of the following toppings is not listed on the menu?

A ham

B sausage

C bacon

D olives

2 According to the menu, which of the following items costs the most?

F a small Super Special pizza

G a medium vegetarian pizza

H a large cheese pizza

J a large pepperoni pizza

3 At which of the following times can pizza be delivered from Jill's Pizza?

A 3:30 P.M.

B 5:00 P.M.

C 5:00 A.M.

D 11:30 A.M.

4 What is the main idea of this selection?

F Pizza restaurants tend to offer many kinds of toppings.

G Some menus list food items according to price.

H Vegetarians are people who do not want to eat meat.

J Restaurants have menus so people know what can be ordered.

5 Why did the author include the menu from Jill's Pizza?

_____

_____

_____

_____

_____

_____

Name _____

Read the selection. Then answer the questions that follow.

The Life of Robert Louis Stevenson

Robert Louis Stevenson was a writer best known for his books *Treasure Island* and *The Strange Case of Dr. Jekyll and Mr. Hyde.* Born in Edinburgh, Scotland, in 1850, Stevenson suffered from poor health at a young age. Although his health made school difficult, he was an excellent reader. At the age of seventeen, Stevenson entered Edinburgh University, where he began studying to become an engineer and then switched to the study of law.

As a university student he began to write and to experiment with different styles of writing. Although he passed his law exams in 1875, Stevenson never practiced law. Instead he traveled to France and other places to improve his health and devoted himself to writing. Stevenson's life was marked by romance, including his marriage to an American woman, Fanny Osbourne, and his travels to the United States and the South Seas. The time line below shows some of the major events in Stevenson's life.

After publishing his novels during the 1880s, Stevenson became a well-known writer who was recognized wherever he went. In addition to writing novels, Stevenson wrote poems, essays, and letters. Popular and successful during his time, Stevenson remains a favorite with readers who recognize his books as fast-paced stories with interesting moral themes.

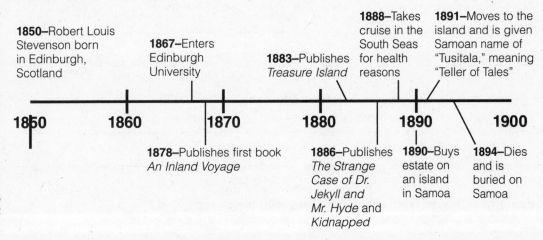

Turn the page.

Answer the questions below.

1 **Which of the following did Stevenson do in 1890?**

   A He began studying at Edinburgh University.

   B He married an American, Fanny Osbourne.

   C He wrote and published *Treasure Island*.

   D He bought an estate on a Samoan island.

2 **According to the time line, when did Stevenson's career as a writer most likely begin?**

   F 1867

   G 1878

   H 1888

   J 1891

3 **What information does the time line provide?**

   A the order of events in Stevenson's life

   B a reason for the reader to read *Treasure Island*

   C the location of Samoa on a map

   D the plot of *The Strange Case of Dr. Jekyll and Mr. Hyde*

4 **What is the main idea of this selection?**

_____

_____

_____

_____

_____

5 **How is this time line different from other time lines you have seen?**

_____

_____

_____

Name _____

Read the selection. Then answer the questions that follow.

Going to the Zoo

A zoo is a park where live animals are kept so that people can see them and scientists can study the animals. Zoos also hold classes and events to teach people about different types of animals. For example, in some classes, students learn about what animals eat, how they sleep, and their other behaviors. Some animals you'll find in a zoo are lions, monkeys, and bears.

Most zoos today try to treat the animals with great care and to create living spaces that are like the animals' natural homes. When you visit a zoo, you usually receive a walking map such as the one below.

Maps such as the one below show you where different animals are in the zoo. Most of the time, you will not have time to see everything in the zoo. By looking at the map, you can find your favorite animals and be sure to see them.

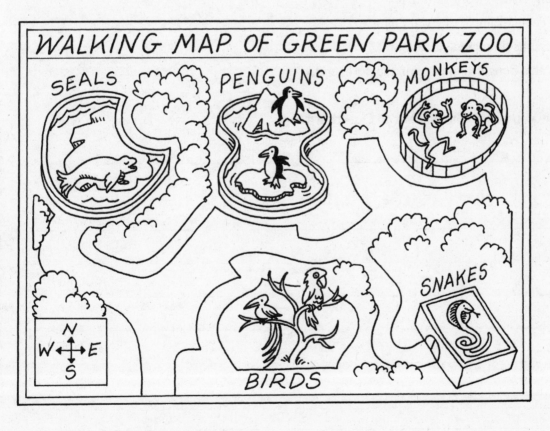

Turn the page.

Answer the questions below.

1 What does the author most likely intend the reader to do after reading this selection?

A become a zoo sponsor

B see zoos as places to learn

C compare zoos in nearby cities

D apply to volunteer at a zoo

2 Which of the following animals are directly south of the monkeys?

F birds

G penguins

H lions

J snakes

3 Why did the author most likely include a walking map of a zoo?

A to prevent visitors from getting lost

B to provide an example of a walking map

C to discuss the arrangement of zoos

D to show that penguins are kept in the north end

4 Explain how you chose your answer to Question 1.

_____

_____

_____

_____

_____

_____

_____

_____

_____

Name _____

Read the selection. Then answer the questions that follow.

The Water Cycle

Our planet has a certain amount of water, which keeps moving around in a process called the water cycle. The water cycle has four main stages: evaporation and transpiration, condensation, precipitation, and collection. You can see the four stages of the water cycle in the diagram below.

Evaporation takes place when the sun heats the water in oceans, rivers, and lakes, turning the water into water vapor, which enters the air. If you have seen steam rising from a bath or pond, you have seen evaporation happen. Water also moves into the air through transpiration, which happens when plants give off water from their leaves.

Evaporation and transpiration are followed by condensation. In the condensation stage, water vapor in the air gets colder and becomes liquid water, which creates clouds. After a while, the clouds become so heavy with water that the air cannot hold any more water. At that point the next phase, called precipitation, occurs. Precipitation is the same thing as raining, snowing, sleeting, or hailing. In this stage, water goes back to the Earth, with the rain, sleet, hail, or snow falling on land and bodies of water.

After the water falls back to the Earth, the phase called collection begins. The Earth collects the water, which travels over the planet, flowing in rivers to the ocean and moving as groundwater underneath the land. The sun continues to shine on bodies of water such as oceans, turning the water into vapor and beginning the water cycle again.

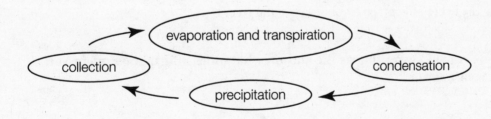

Turn the page.

Answer the questions below.

1 **Which of the following best describes the author's purpose?**

A to persuade people to collect rainwater

B to urge people to limit water usage

C to show how evaporation has changed over time

D to describe the stages of the water cycle

2 **Which of the following best describes the author's tone in the selection?**

F scientific

G amusing

H bossy

J angry

3 **According to the diagram, which stage follows condensation?**

A transpiration

B collection

C evaporation

D precipitation

4 **Why did the author most likely include the diagram?**

F to show the circle of the water cycle

G to show differences among types of precipitation

H to explain how water collects in clouds

J to explain how the cycle affects the level of lakes and rivers

5 **If you had the same reason for writing as the author, what other information might you include? Explain your answer.**

_____

_____

_____

_____

_____

Name _____

Read the selection. Then answer the questions that follow.

What Ladybugs Do

The ladybug is a type of beetle. Also called the lady beetle or ladybird beetle, ladybugs are liked by farmers because they help plants grow. Most ladybugs eat insects that harm plants. Farmers buy ladybugs to keep insects from destroying their crops. Ladybugs have huge appetites because they need to eat a lot of insects to grow and lay eggs. Some ladybugs eat hundreds of insects every day. The insects they eat include aphids, which eat plants such as roses.

The ladybug is less than half an inch in length and is rounded on top and flat on the bottom. Most ladybugs are red or orange with black, white, or yellow spots. However, some ladybugs are completely black. Having a small head and short legs, some ladybugs have seven spots while others have more or fewer spots. There are about six thousand different kinds of ladybugs. The diagram below shows what a ladybug generally looks like.

In the winter, some ladybugs live in houses. Some live under leaves, rocks, or bark, where they hibernate (sleep) all winter. Others spend the winter in the mountains, and many ladybugs are collected from the mountains. After being collected, the ladybugs are sent to people who want them. Farmers release the ladybugs on crops and hope they will stay.

In the spring, you can find ladybugs in vegetable and flower gardens. If you want to study a ladybug, try using old bottles or containers to collect them. You might also place a piece of paper towel or leaf inside the container so that the ladybug has something to hold on to during the trip to your home.

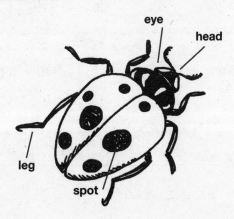

Turn the page.

Answer the questions below.

1 The author's purpose in writing this selection was to

A persuade farmers to buy beetles.

B express an opinion about insects.

C inform the reader about ladybugs.

D compare different types of ladybugs.

2 According to the diagram, a ladybug's head is

F smaller than its body.

G usually red or orange.

H the size of a pencil eraser.

J covered with fur.

3 The author included a diagram of a ladybug most likely to show

A the different parts of a ladybug.

B how ladybugs eat.

C one color ladybugs can be.

D how few parts a ladybug has.

4 What clues from the selection helped you choose your answer to Question 1? Explain.

_____

_____

_____

_____

_____

5 If you had the same reason for writing as the author, what additional graphic sources would you be most likely to include?

_____

_____

_____

_____

Name _____

Read the selection. Then answer the questions that follow.

Bandana of the Future

Since the days of cowboys, bandanas have been in style. Cowboys used them to block dust and sun, handle hot pots, and even as an arm sling if needed. In more modern times, they've mostly been worn as head scarves. The early ones were red and made of silk, cotton, or linen. Modern bandanas come in many colors, patterns, and materials.

The bandana of the future is here. Not a plain square or triangle tied in a knot—this is a tube of material that stretches and can be worn in a variety of ways. If you twist the tube in the middle and fit one end over the outside of the other, you have a hat! If you carefully roll the opening at one end all the way down, you have a headband! Pull the tube over your head, and you have a neck warmer!

Turn the page.

Answer the questions below.

1 A cowboy picking up a pot would *most likely* use his bandana because

A the sun made it hard to see.

B his arm had been hurt.

C a dust storm blinded him.

D the handle was too hot.

2 Based on the selection, why have bandanas *probably* stayed popular?

F They can always be worn as headscarves.

G Updates keep making them fashionable.

H They can be made of different materials.

J People always want to look like cowboys.

3 The author *mostly* wants the reader to

A try to use a bandana in the same ways that the cowboys did.

B remember the first wearers of bandanas were the cowboys.

C feel curious enough about the tube bandana to go get one.

D ask if their friends have bandanas of silk, cotton, or linen.

4 Which feature of "the bandana of the future" enables you to use it as different items of clothing? Explain your answer.

_____

_____

_____

_____

_____

_____

_____

_____

_____

_____

Name _____

Read the selection. Then answer the questions that follow.

Kudzu, Superhated Superhero

Kudzu may be the only plant able to leap a tall building in a single bound. It can grow up to 60 feet a year. Many Southerners hate this useful but greedy vine, which was brought to the U.S. from Japan in 1876. If you live in or have driven through the Southeast, you've probably seen what looks like a sculpture garden along the roadside. The forms of trees and ruined buildings, softened by layers of deep green kudzu, are a beautiful sight—at once both prehistoric and futuristic.

Many plants and animals brought from one country into another to solve a problem have instead become problems. Cane toads from Central and South America were introduced into Australia in 1935. They were brought in to control Australia's cane beetles, a pest of sugarcane crops. Unfortunately, the cane toads couldn't jump high enough to catch the cane beetles. Instead, they began eating everything else . . . and growing in numbers. The toads have had a serious impact on populations of native snakes, lizards, and birds.

Through the early twentieth century, people used kudzu to add fast-growing leafy shade to porches. Through 1935, it was used for cattle grazing, and, for about the next twenty years, to keep soil from washing away from rain and floodwater. Mid-century, people began to get sick of it. The vines grow as much as a foot per day in summer. They can choke whole forests by blocking sunlight. The U.S. Department of Agriculture classified kudzu as a weed in 1972. Several modern weavers use kudzu to make rugged, lovely baskets, but overall the "miracle vine" has, alas, become "the vine that ate the South."

Turn the page.

Answer the questions below.

1 **In the first paragraph, what is the author's main purpose?**

   A to impress readers with images of kudzu's power and beauty

   B to urge readers to work to save kudzu from southerners

   C to argue that strength is much more important than usefulness

   D to confuse readers with the image of a vine as a superhero

2 **For what reason were the South American toads brought to Australia?**

   F to keep weeds out of the fields of sugarcane

   G to prevent their species from dying out

   H to eat up the native snakes, lizards, and birds

   J to lower the high number of cane beetles

3 **What impact did cane toads have on Australia?**

   A Their expansion made it a model for saving endangered species.

   B They kept beetles and other pests from killing the crops.

   C Their population grew and threatened the native populations.

   D They greatly increased the amount of sugarcane produced.

4 **Kudzu was used on Southern porches to create shade quickly. How might this use of kudzu cause problems?**

_____

_____

_____

_____

_____

5 **Explain why cane toads turned out to be a problem rather than a solution in Australia.**

_____

_____

_____

_____

_____

Name _____

Read the selection. Then answer the questions that follow.

Where It's Always 98.6 Degrees

The human body does a few uncomfortable but amazing things to maintain its central temperature at 98.6 degrees. For example, on hot days the body sweats to keep its temperature from rising. This process is called *evaporative cooling*. You can investigate this process without leaving your chair. Lick the back of your hand. Now blow gently on it. Do you feel the cool sensation?

Humidity—how much water is in the air—affects how long sweat stays on your skin. If the humidity is low, the air is relatively dry. This means there's room in the air for your sweat, so the sweat will dry quickly. If the humidity's high, there's a lot of water in the air. This means the sweat remains on your skin, so you feel clammy and sticky.

Likewise, in winter, the body does some extraordinary things to stay warm. As the temperature drops, blood vessels expand and blood pressure rises. The tiny muscles at the base of each hair contract to trap warm air next to skin. You may also start shivering. Shivering can create a surprising five-fold increase in internal body heat. The heat is delivered to the center part of your body to protect your internal organs. At the same time, the blood supply to hands, feet, and nose is limited. That's why those parts grow numb.

The body responds to summer and winter extremes with signals that it's working to keep you alive and well. If you stop sweating on a really hot day and suddenly feel cold, seek help. On a really cold day, if shivering suddenly stops, you're too cold and need to warm up.

Turn the page.

Answer the questions below.

1 Based on the selection, if you are sweating on a hot day and then you suddenly stop sweating and feel cold, what has *most likely* just happened?

A Your rising blood pressure has increased too much.

B Shivering has lowered your internal temperature.

C Your body temperature climbed to an unhealthy level.

D High humidity caused all your sweat to evaporate.

2 According to the selection, we feel sticky and clammy when we are outside on a humid day because

F our internal temperature is higher than 98.6 degrees.

G water in the air mixes in with our sweat.

H the outdoor temperature is higher than 98.6 degrees.

J water in the air lets sweat stay on our skin.

3 What causes hands and feet to go numb when you are out in the winter cold?

A tightened muscles

B expanding blood vessels

C excessive shivering

D limited blood supply

4 Based on information in the selection, how would the air feel on your skin when you climbed out of a swimming pool on a hot, dry day? Explain your answer.

_____

_____

_____

5 In this selection, how does the author hope to persuade readers to view sweating and shivering?

_____

_____

_____

Name _____

Read the selection. Then answer the questions that follow.

Koalas

The koala is an animal that lives along the eastern coast of Australia. Sometimes called *koala bears,* koalas are not really bears but marsupials. These animals with pouches feed their babies with milk. When koalas are born, they live in their mothers' pouches.

Koalas live in trees, which protect them from other animals and provide them with leaves to eat. Koalas generally eat eucalyptus tree leaves, eating one to three pounds every day. Koalas have very strong claws and two thumbs on each of their front feet to help them grip tree branches. Koalas also have soft gray fur, large faces, and furry ears.

Koalas depend on trees in order to survive. Even though koalas generally live to be about twenty years old, there are far fewer of them now than there were before. There were once millions of koalas, but now there are only a few hundred thousand. Disease and people cutting down so many trees have caused the decrease. Some people are now planting trees to make good places for koalas to live.

Where Koalas Live

Koalas live along the eastern coast of Australia.

Turn the page.

Answer the questions below.

1 Which of the following is a generalization based on the second paragraph?

A Koalas mostly eat eucalyptus tree leaves.

B Koalas can usually be found in the mountains.

C Most koalas live in trees to avoid dogs and cats.

D Some koalas are members of the bear family.

2 Which of the following clue words helped you choose your answer to Question 1?

F also

G very

H now

J generally

3 What generalization can you make from looking at the map?

A Because there are fewer trees now, there are fewer koalas.

B All koalas live along the coast of eastern Australia.

C Koalas are the only animals that live in trees.

D Most koalas have roomy pouches.

4 Make a generalization based on the information in the last paragraph. Which clue words in the paragraph helped you make your generalization?

_____

_____

_____

_____

_____

_____

_____

_____

_____

Name _____

Read the selection. Then answer the questions that follow.

Measuring Rainfall

Chances are that you know what rain is, but what about rainfall? Rainfall means all the water that falls on a particular area in any form, including rain, snow, hail, sleet, frost, and dew. Rainfall is very important to people everywhere, since we depend on water to grow crops, to drink, and to bathe. Because water is so important, scientists like to measure the amount of rainfall in different areas of the world each year.

The amount of rainfall in different parts of the world varies greatly, from as much as 472 inches each year on Mount Waialeale in Hawaii to as little as less than one inch in Arica, Chile. In most places, people, animals, and crops need about twenty inches of rainfall per year in order to do well. The bar graph below shows some amounts of rainfall in different places.

Not all rainfall helps people to grow crops and do other important tasks. For example, rain that falls on steep hills or runs off land that has been paved over, such as highways, is not generally useful. Rain that falls on pavement usually becomes polluted and is not fit for drinking. When this happens, people have to find other ways of getting their supply of water. Too much rainfall can also be a problem, since the excess rain washes away land and can remove minerals from the soil.

If you want to measure rainfall in your area, you should use a clean container with a flat bottom and straight sides and place the container where it will catch the rain or other forms of precipitation. When you measure the amount of water in the container, use a thin ruler or measure the water level from the outside of the container.

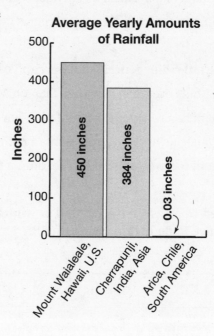

Average Yearly Amounts of Rainfall

Turn the page.

- -

Answer the questions below.

1 **Which of the following is a generalization based on the second paragraph?**

  A Arica, Chile, is one of the rainiest places on the planet.

  B In some parts of the world, it rains all the time.

  C Measuring rainfall can be difficult in places such as Hawaii.

  D People need about twenty inches of rainfall per year to do well.

2 **Which of the following clue words helped you choose your answer to Question 1?**

  F most

  G as much as

  H since

  J some

3 **Which of the following is a generalization based on the third paragraph?**

  A Most rain falls on steep hills or on paved roads.

  B In many places, too much rain falls, causing mudslides.

  C Rain that falls on pavement usually becomes unfit for drinking.

  D Usually, it rains more in the United States than in South America.

4 **Which of the following generalizations can you make from looking at the bar graph?**

  F More rain falls every year in Arica than on Mount Waialeale.

  G Cherrapunji receives the most rainfall of any place on Earth.

  H Mount Waialeale usually receives more rainfall than Arica.

  J Cherrapunji receives most of its rain during the monsoon season.

5 **If you wanted to measure the rainfall in winter in a place where it's cold enough to snow, what might you have to do before measuring the level?**

_____

_____

_____

_____

_____

_____

Name _____

Read the selection. Then answer the questions that follow.

Counting Sockeye Salmon

A salmon is a type of fish that lives in many parts of the Pacific Northwest, such as the city of Seattle in Washington State. Salmon are known for swimming from the ocean upstream in rivers to get to places where they can spawn, or lay their eggs. One type of salmon is the sockeye. This type of salmon can be picked out by its coloring and other markings.

When adult sockeye return to rivers to begin their journey upstream, they are usually silvery in color. However, as they travel, these fish begin to turn brighter colors, showing a pattern of red on their bodies and green on their heads and tails. Unlike other salmon, sockeye usually have no large spots on their backs and tails, and their eyes are gold in color. Sockeye also have no silver color on their tails after they begin to swim upstream. They also have small teeth.

As with all types of salmon, most sockeye spawn only at a certain time of year, and for the sockeye that time is the summer. The following chart shows how many sockeye pass through the Ballard Locks in Seattle, which is one of the places the fish swim through on their way to the spawning ground. The chart below shows the total numbers of sockeye that went through the locks every other day at the end of June 2004.

By reading charts such as this one, you can figure out when you are likely to see sockeye salmon swimming upstream. It is quite a sight to watch thousands of brightly colored fish swimming all at once against a river's flow!

**Sockeye Salmon Counts
at the Ballard Locks for June 2004**

Date	Daily Count
June 12	1,801
June 14	1,492
June 16	2,710
June 18	2,325
June 20	4,704
June 22	5,452
June 24	7,108
June 26	7,089
June 28	11,184
June 30	10,204

Turn the page.

Answer the questions below.

1 **Which of the following is a generalization based on the second paragraph?**

   A All salmon live in the ocean for most of their lives.

   B When sockeye salmon swim upstream, they turn bright colors.

   C Unlike other salmon, sockeye swim downstream to lay their eggs.

   D You can usually identify sockeye salmon by their green stripes.

2 **Which of the following is a generalization based on the third paragraph?**

   F Sockeye salmon only spawn in late August and September.

   G There are more sockeye salmon than any other kind.

   H The Ballard Locks is a favorite tourist spot in Seattle.

   J Most sockeye spawn only in the summer.

3 **Which of the following clue words in paragraph three helped you choose your answer to Question 2?**

   A most

   B following

   C only

   D because

4 **What generalization can you make from reading the chart?**

_____

_____

_____

_____

5 **What facts from the chart support your generalization?**

_____

_____

_____

Name _____

Read the selection. Then answer the questions that follow.

Lyall's Quiet Day

Lyall was a sixth grader who lived with his parents and his younger brother and sisters, Marcus, Lenora, and Tina. Lyall liked his brother and two sisters very much, but sometimes he got tired of all the talking. So one day he decided to not talk to anyone for the rest of the day.

Before he quit talking, Lyall told his parents that he was going to be silent until the next day. Then he told Lenora, Marcus, and Tina about the plan, and although Lenora resisted the idea, she and the others agreed not to speak to Lyall until then.

For the rest of the day, whenever he wanted something, Lyall either made a sign with his hands or wrote something down. Pretty soon, his whole family joined in on his quiet plan, and instead of talking, they wrote notes to each other. Lyall found that he often wanted to talk to his brother and sisters, but he enjoyed the notes and thought the silent day had been an interesting experiment.

Turn the page.

Answer the questions below.

1 Why did Lyall want to have a quiet day?

  A to do his homework

  B to practice his hand gestures

  C to take a break from talking

  D to see what writing notes was like

2 Which of the following best describes Lyall?

  F He tends to ask lots of questions.

  G He often forgets where he put something.

  H He knows how to make a plan work.

  J He is well liked by his brother and sisters.

3 Based on the selection, which generalization can you make?

  A Family members' experiments are always useful.

  B Lyall's family members never get on his nerves.

  C Every member of Lyall's family talks way too much.

  D Lyall's family members usually support each other.

4 Did Lyall's family enjoy the quiet day? Explain your answer.

_____

_____

_____

_____

_____

_____

_____

_____

_____

Name _____

Read the selection. Then answer the questions that follow.

Rolando and Blue Fairy

Rolando and Steve were outside playing catch in front of Rolando's house when they suddenly heard a delicate voice say, "Hello there! Please, help me!" Rolando turned to see where the unusual voice was coming from, and soon he spotted the source: a tiny blue fairy trapped beneath a spiky branch that had fallen on the ground.

"I can help you," said Rolando, as he walked over to the fairy and lifted the branch. "Are you hurt?" he asked.

"No, I am perfectly fine, but thank you for asking," said the fairy, brushing bits of leaves and dried bark off herself. "I'm quite indebted to you for your attentive intervention, and I would like to grant you the standard three wishes."

Rolando was a decisive person used to making quick decisions, so he didn't hesitate for long and said, "For my first wish, I'd like a new baseball mitt, since this one is deteriorating and about to fall apart."

"Done!" said the fairy, and immediately a shimmering, new baseball mitt appeared in Rolando's hands. "What next?"

"Now, I would like a new mitt for Steve, since he needs a new one too," he said.

"Very well," said the fairy, and instantly another mitt appeared for Steve, who thanked Rolando. "And for your final wish?"

"For my third wish, I'd like every house in the neighborhood to be a different shade of blue, so that I remember this magical time," said Rolando.

"Well, that's quite unusual," said the fairy, but she granted the wish, and suddenly all the houses were different shades of blue. Then she disappeared, waving good-by.

"Thank you—it's beautiful," cried Rolando, and he and Steve ran through the neighborhood admiring all the blue houses. They remember the time of the three wishes every now and then.

Turn the page.

Answer the questions below.

1 **How does Rolando appear to feel about the way he used his wishes?**

A worried the neighbors may dislike their blue houses

B proud he had asked the fairy for something unusual

C troubled because he could have asked for other things

D satisfied with the three good choices that he had made

2 **Which of the following supports the conclusion that Rolando was a thoughtful person?**

F The houses in the neighborhood needed new paint.

G He made his three wishes very quickly.

H He does not ask for additional wishes.

J His second wish was a gift for his friend Steve.

3 **Why did Rolando wish for all the houses to be blue?**

A He wanted to remember meeting the fairy.

B Blue was his favorite color.

C His own house was already blue.

D Blue reminded him of the sky and the ocean.

4 **Which information in the selection expresses a generalization?**

F Rolando and Steve were outside playing catch in front of Rolando's house.

G Rolando was a decisive person used to making quick decisions.

H I'd like every house in the neighborhood to be a different shade of blue.

J She granted the wish and then she disappeared, waving good-by.

5 **How much time has probably passed since Rolando's experience with the blue fairy? Explain how you know.**

_____

_____

_____

_____

_____

Read the selection. Then answer the questions that follow.

Susan Meets a Dolphin

Susan loved the ocean more than anything else, and she liked to spend the bulk of her summer vacation swimming and jumping waves at the beach. Since her family lived on a tropical island only a few blocks from the ocean, she could swim as much as she wanted to as long as she accomplished her various chores for the day.

One sweltering day in August, Susan and her best friend, Ryan, were swimming at the beach as usual, when suddenly Susan felt something glide by her foot. "Very funny," she said to Ryan, but as she turned around to face him, she realized that he was over ten feet away.

While she was turning around in the water, she also heard Ryan say, "Hey, what was that?" They both became a bit startled when they saw a gray fin skimming above the surface of the water. However, right after seeing the fin, they saw a sleek dolphin jump through the water.

"It's jumping waves like us," said Susan gleefully. "Let's follow it!"

Ryan and Susan swam after the dolphin, knowing that they would have to swim swiftly to keep up. Pretty soon they lost sight of the dolphin, since it was a much faster swimmer than they were, and they stopped to catch their breath in a cove around the bend from where they had started. "I've never seen this cove before. It's lovely," said Susan, as she admired the seaweed moving under the water.

"It's full of unusual coral," said Ryan. "It's not like anything else around here."

For the rest of the day, Susan and Ryan explored the new cove, looking at the varieties of coral. Susan felt happy that the dolphin had led them to this new ocean spot.

Turn the page.

Answer the questions below.

1 **Based on the story, which of the following best describes Susan's athletic ability?**

   A She is a strong swimmer and physically active.

   B She prefers field sports such as soccer and hockey.

   C She prefers to sit and do quiet activities.

   D She is a great diver but not a very good swimmer.

2 **What conclusion does Susan draw in the second paragraph?**

   F A dolphin has grazed her foot.

   G The dolphin will lead them somewhere.

   H Ryan has played a trick on her.

   J They will find the hidden cove that day.

3 **Which clue words in the second paragraph suggest that Susan and Ryan swim nearly every day in August?**

   A one sweltering day

   B were swimming

   C at the beach

   D as usual

4 **What do the details in the story suggest about Susan?**

_____

_____

_____

_____

_____

_____

5 **Why did Susan and Ryan explore the cove?**

_____

_____

_____

Name _____

Read the selection. Then answer the questions that follow.

The Planet Venus

Venus is the second planet from the sun, and it lies between Earth and the planet Mercury. One of the brightest objects in the night sky, Venus is outshone only by the moon. Venus is also the closest planet to us, and it is like Earth in its dense and rocky surface. Like other planets, Venus travels around the sun, taking 225 Earth days to complete one full journey.

Venus's atmosphere is made up mostly of the gas carbon dioxide. Because of this gas, the planet is very hot, with temperatures reaching 864 degrees Fahrenheit! The gas traps heat from the sun, keeping the heat from rising back into space.

People have been watching Venus for thousands of years. In about 3000 B.C., people in Babylonia, China, and other places recorded seeing the planet. The scientist Galileo's discovery of Venus's phases in 1610 supported the then new idea that the planets travel around the sun.

Turn the page.

Answer the questions below.

1 The topic of the second paragraph is

   A how far Venus is from the planet Jupiter.

   B the atmosphere and temperatures on Venus.

   C how to spot Venus in the night sky.

   D how long it takes Venus to circle the sun.

2 Which of the following states the main idea of the third paragraph?

   F Venus is one of the planets closest to the sun and is like Earth.

   G People in Central America were the first to record seeing Venus.

   H Galileo discovered the phases of Venus in 1610.

   J People have been watching Venus for thousands of years.

3 Which of the following events most likely occurred before Galileo discovered Venus's phases?

   A The United States sent the spacecraft *Mariner* to Venus.

   B The Soviet spacecraft *Venera* took photos of Venus's surface.

   C Astronomers discovered the planets Neptune and Uranus.

   D The Babylonians and the Chinese recorded seeing Venus.

4 Based on the selection, what makes Venus most unlike Earth when it comes to supporting human or familiar forms of animal life?

Name _____

Read the selection. Then answer the questions that follow.

Zora Neale Hurston

Zora Neale Hurston was an American writer and anthropologist who was a part of the Harlem Renaissance, a movement that took place in New York in the 1920s and 1930s. During the Harlem Renaissance, many African American writers, musicians, and artists created works celebrating the life of black Americans. The writers in this group who created important works showing a new side to American life included Langston Hughes, Jean Toomer, and Claude McKay. Hurston was a key figure in the movement, and like some other Harlem Renaissance writers, she drew on folk stories as well as more traditional forms of writing.

Born in 1891 in Alabama, Hurston grew up there and in a Florida town called Eatonville. She lived in New York City during the Harlem Renaissance, working with other writers, including poet Langston Hughes. She attended Howard University from 1923 to 1924, and graduated in 1928 from Barnard College in New York, studying anthropology, the study of people and their cultures. After pursuing anthropology as a graduate student at Columbia University in New York, she did field studies in folklore in African American communities in the South. Her book *Mules and Men* describes the culture of a black community in Florida.

Hurston is known widely for her novels, especially *Their Eyes Were Watching God,* which was published in 1937. She published her first novel, *Jonah's Gourd Vine,* in 1934, and the book received praise for its realistic portrayal of African American life. Readers and scholars also admire her autobiography *Dust Tracks on a Road.* In the last twenty years, Hurston's work has gained a lot of attention, and some of her work has been published for the first time, including stories in her collection *The Complete Stories,* which appeared in 1995.

Turn the page.

Answer the questions below.

1 **Which of the following best states the main idea of the first paragraph?**

   A The Harlem Renaissance took place during the 1920s and 1930s.

   B Zora Neale Hurston wrote a play with the poet Langston Hughes.

   C Alabama and Florida produced the well-known writer Zora Neale Hurston.

   D Zora Neale Hurston was an important figure in the Harlem Renaissance.

2 **Which of the following best states the main idea of the last paragraph?**

   F Hurston is best known for her novels and nonfiction.

   G Readers and scholars prefer Hurston's nonfiction.

   H Hurston's short stories were not published during her lifetime.

   J Only in the last twenty years has Hurston's fiction appeared.

3 **Which of the following details supports the main idea of the second paragraph?**

   A *Mules and Men* is written like a story or narrative.

   B *Mules and Men* strongly reflected Hurston's area of interest.

   C Anthropologists thought *Mules and Men* was unscientific.

   D Hurston did not finish her graduate degree in anthropology.

4 **Which of the following happened before Hurston studied anthropology?**

   F She attended Howard University.

   G She did anthropological field studies in the South.

   H She participated in the Harlem Renaissance.

   J *Dust Tracks on a Road* was published.

5 **How might Hurston's anthropological book *Mules and Men* have prepared her to play a role in the Harlem Renaissance?**

_____

_____

_____

_____

_____

Name _____

Read the selection. Then answer the questions that follow.

What Is a Tardigrade?

In many places on Earth, you can find an amazing creature called the tardigrade, which is also known as the "water bear" because it resembles a very small bear. The term *tardigrade* includes about 350 types of tiny invertebrates—animals without backbones. A highly adaptable creature, the water bear lives in sand, the ocean, wet moss, rivers, and on flowering plants.

Less than one millimeter in size and simple in structure, the tardigrade has a head and a torso made up of four parts with a short limb attached to each part. The limbs usually end in sharp claws, and plant-eating water bears eat by using sharp points near their mouths called *stylets* to pierce plant cells and special tubes to suck out the juice. Some tardigrades hunt other tiny creatures and eat meat.

Water bears are unusually adaptable. They can withstand being completely dried out for long periods of time and can stand extremely low or high temperatures. For example, some tardigrades can handle being exposed to temperatures as low as –112 degrees Fahrenheit for several hours and still come to life and move about when they are brought back to room temperature. Scientists have determined that these creatures go into a special state in which their physical processes slow way down, and that enables them to survive being completely frozen!

Because of their unusual hardiness, tardigrades are found everywhere from the tropical forests to the Arctic Ocean. You may even be able to find some of these creatures in your neighborhood. Try looking at some moss or lichen under a microscope to see whether any of these strange creatures are present.

Turn the page.

Answer the questions below.

1 The main idea of this selection is that

   A people should make efforts to protect tardigrades.

   B tardigrades are very small animals.

   C the habitat of the tardigrade is widely varied.

   D tardigrades are very tough creatures.

2 Which of the following does the selection mainly suggest?

   F Very few meat-eating tardigrades have *stylets*.

   G All tardigrades can survive extreme temperatures.

   H There may be more than 350 types of tardigrade.

   J Some tardigrades can withstand high heat, others extreme cold.

3 Where does the selection suggest you look for tardigrades?

   A sand

   B ocean

   C moss

   D river

4 According to the second paragraph, what does a tardigrade do after piercing a plant with its stylets?

_____

_____

_____

_____

_____

5 After a tardigrade is exposed to very high heat, what, other than a more moderate temperature, is necessary for it to become "alive" again?

_____

_____

_____

_____

Name _____

Read the selection. Then answer the questions that follow.

Nora and the Magic Box

Nora was a seventh grader who often helped her neighbor Ms. Bacho tend her garden by removing weeds and digging holes. One day while Nora was digging holes to plant carrot seeds, she hit something hard with the spade she was using. Looking down, Nora saw something metallic shining through the dirt, and she carefully dug a little more until she uncovered the mysterious object, which turned out to be a metallic box.

Although the box appeared to be ordinary, when Nora lifted the box, it began to tremble like a wet cat, and then suddenly the box's lid flew open. Inside the box Nora saw two pieces of paper, which were exactly the same size and shape. However, one of the pieces of paper was green, while the other one was orange.

Nora cautiously lifted the green paper, which turned into a row of bright, green pea plants. When she picked up the orange paper, it changed into a beautiful orange tree. Nora was delighted with the changes, although she wasn't sure if Ms. Bacho would believe what had happened.

Turn the page.

Answer the questions below.

1 At the beginning of the second paragraph, why was the box compared to a cat?

A Both would be old.

B Both would be wet.

C Both would tremble and shiver.

D Both would be mysterious.

2 The two pieces of paper were different in

F size.

G shape.

H texture.

J color.

3 Which of the following words best describes Nora?

A helpful

B mournful

C studious

D tiny

4 How are Nora and Ms. Bacho alike?

_____

_____

_____

_____

_____

_____

_____

_____

_____

_____

Name _____

Read the selection. Then answer the questions that follow.

A Tale of Two Dogs

Sarah was a fourth grader, and one of her jobs was to take care of the family dog, Roger. Taking care of Roger meant feeding him twice a day, giving him baths, and walking him in the morning and in the evening. Sarah thought Roger was a great dog, so taking care of him was enjoyable and easy for her.

One evening, Sarah was walking Roger around the neighborhood when they came upon another owner and his dog. This was not an unusual occurrence in itself—Sarah frequently met other people walking their pets around the town. However, this time, Sarah and the other person, who was a serious-looking boy about Sarah's age, stopped to observe each other, because their dogs looked almost identical.

Like Roger, the other dog was medium-sized and had bristly brown fur, enormous white paws, and a white tail. The other dog, whose name it turned out was Robert, had a similar black nose and a zigzagging streak of black fur down his back. Most strikingly, the two dogs acted similarly—when Roger excitedly turned around in a little circle, so did Robert. When Robert did a somersault in the air, so did Roger. "It's like they're twins," said Sarah.

"Yes, how strange," said the boy, who introduced himself as Oliver. "I wonder if we could even tell them apart."

Then all of a sudden, Roger and Robert started barking at a squirrel that was running up a tree, and Sarah and Oliver started laughing because they realized that the dogs were different after all. Unlike Roger, who had a short, low-pitched bark, Robert had a bark that was high-pitched and squeaky. "Robert's bark sounds like squeezing a rubber duck," said Oliver.

"It does," said Sarah, and she went home to tell her mom about the meeting of the two dogs.

Turn the page.

Answer the questions below.

1 **Roger and Robert were alike in that they both**

A had zigzagging streaks of black fur.

B liked to catch balls in their front paws.

C went for walks twice a day around the neighborhood.

D had lived with their owners for three years.

2 **The two dogs differed in the way they**

F looked.

G moved.

H growled.

J barked.

3 **Sarah and Oliver are alike in that they both—**

A went to the same school.

B walked their dogs around the neighborhood.

C trained dogs for dog shows.

D ignored dog owners walking medium-sized dogs.

4 **Which of the following words best describes Sarah?**

F cautious

G responsible

H lucky

J homesick

5 **What did Oliver compare Robert's bark to and why?**

_____

_____

_____

_____

_____

_____

Name _____

Read the selection. Then answer the questions that follow.

Eldon and Jay Solve a Problem

Once there were two twin brothers named Eldon and Jay, who lived in a big city in Europe. Eldon and Jay were identical in nearly every way, as both teenagers had wavy dark hair, round eyeglasses, and brilliant smiles. They talked in the same confident manner, and they even had similar styles of dancing, walking, and gesturing. People frequently got the two of them confused.

However, there was one small difference between the two twins. Unlike Jay, whose favorite pastime was making pastries, Eldon couldn't stand eating anything sweet. Ever since he'd been an infant, Eldon had refused to eat cookies, cake, candy, or any dessert. Jay did not particularly like eating sweet things, but he loved to bake them, and whenever he was baking, Eldon would go to his room and practice playing the trombone.

Eldon had played the trombone for a year, but he was still a beginner, and in Jay's opinion, Eldon was not the greatest trombone player. One day when Jay was in the kitchen making a batch of muffins, he heard Eldon practice playing scales on the trombone. "What an awful noise," said Jay to himself. "It sounds like an elephant weeping."

Jay went up to Eldon's room and said, "Could you please play more quietly while I'm trying to bake?"

Eldon was a little taken aback by his brother's polite request, but he said, "I see my playing is disturbing your concentration. However, I also find it hard to be in the kitchen when you're baking, since, as you know, I can't stand to be around sugar. Maybe we can figure out a solution together."

The twins sat down and worked out a plan in which Eldon would only practice the trombone in the practice room at school, and Jay would apprentice himself to a baker and only bake at the bakery. Each of the twins found that this arrangement worked quite well.

Turn the page.

Answer the questions below.

1 Eldon and Jay are different in that

A only Jay seems very confident.

B Jay smiled a lot, whereas Eldon did not smile much.

C Eldon dislikes sweet things, whereas Jay likes to bake pastries.

D Jay enjoys playing the tuba, while Eldon plays the piano.

2 Eldon and Jay are similar in that they both

F eat sweets.

G wear eyeglasses.

H play the trombone.

J have blonde hair.

3 In the third paragraph, what did Jay compare Eldon's trombone playing to?

A a loud pigeon

B a broken cookie

C a lumpy muffin

D a crying elephant

4 If you were in a donut shop and saw one of the twins there having only coffee, which twin would it probably be? Explain your answer.

_____

_____

_____

_____

5 If the twins were strolling down the street together and motioning to get someone's attention at the bus stop, would you probably be able to tell them apart? Why or why not?

_____

_____

_____

Name _____

Read the selection. Then answer the questions that follow.

The Oldest Sport in North America

You might be surprised to learn that the oldest team sport in North America is not football or baseball, but a game called lacrosse. Based on a Native American sport called *baggataway*, the game was taken up by European Canadians in about 1840. These players changed the rules of the sport and called it *lacrosse* because the stick players use looks like a crosier, which is a type of walking stick. The Canadian government made lacrosse the national game in 1867.

Today, the sport is played with a small rubber sponge ball. Players carry and throw the ball using a long-handled stick with a basket at the end of it. As with hockey, two teams try to score points by tossing the ball into a netted goal at the ends of a field. One point is scored for each goal. The sport is fast-paced and exciting to watch, so everyone should see a lacrosse game at least once.

Turn the page.

Answer the questions below.

1 **Which of the following is a statement of fact based on the first paragraph?**

A Few people care that lacrosse was the first team sport in North America.

B Lacrosse changed the rules of the Native American game baggataway.

C Baggataway was too confusing to understand.

D Lacrosse is a more exciting game than baggataway was.

2 **Which of the following contains a statement of opinion in the second paragraph?**

F the first sentence

G the third sentence

H the fourth sentence

J the last sentence

3 **Which of the following reference sources would be most useful to verify the statements of fact in this selection?**

A a map of Canada

B an encyclopedia

C a science textbook

D a dictionary

4 **What is the topic of the second paragraph?**

_____

_____

_____

_____

_____

_____

_____

_____

_____

Name _____

Read the selection. Then answer the questions that follow.

Amelia Earhart: The First Woman to Fly Over the Atlantic

Amelia Earhart was a renowned American aviator (airplane pilot), who became famous for several daring flights. Born in 1897, Earhart worked as a nurse and a social worker after graduating from high school in Chicago. In the early 1920s she learned how to fly a plane, and in 1928 she became the first woman to cross the Atlantic Ocean in a plane, although she was a passenger on that flight.

The 1928 flight was the first of several achievements by Earhart, who went on to set several more records during the 1930s. After crossing the Atlantic as a passenger, Earhart decided to fly across the Atlantic as a pilot by herself, and in 1932 she accomplished that goal, flying solo from Newfoundland, North America, to Ireland in the record time of fourteen hours and fifty-six minutes.

Earhart also wrote books about her remarkable experiences as a pilot. The book she published after the 1932 flight, *The Fun of It,* is a lively account of her journey. She also wrote another book called *20 Hrs., 40 Min.,* which recalls her 1928 flight across the Atlantic.

In 1935 Earhart set another world flying record by becoming the first person to fly alone from Hawaii to California, which was a longer distance than her flight from North America to Ireland. Throughout her career, Earhart sought to create more opportunities for women in the world of aviation (flying), since it was still unusual for women to become pilots at the time.

Today, Earhart is remembered as a bold adventurer, who was at the fore of the first years of international aviation. Her life story is told in many biographies, including *Soaring Wings,* which was written by her husband, the publisher George Palmer Putnam, and was first published in 1939.

Turn the page.

Answer the questions below.

1 Based on the selection, which of the following is a statement of fact?

A Earhart was the most beloved and famous pilot of her time.

B Earhart was the first woman to cross the Atlantic in a plane.

C Earhart should have written more than two books.

D No other early pilots were as brave as Earhart.

2 Based on the selection, which of the following is a statement of opinion?

F Earhart wrote books about her experiences as a pilot.

G The book *20 Hrs., 40 Min.* tells about her 1928 flight.

H Earhart's first book was published in 1931.

J *The Fun of It* is a lively account of one of Earhart's journeys.

3 Which of the following reference sources would be most useful to verify the statement of facts in this selection?

A a dictionary

B a world atlas

C an almanac

D an encyclopedia

4 The main idea of the second paragraph is that—

F Earhart set many records in flight.

G most pilots were men during the 1930s.

H Earhart crossed the Atlantic alone in 1932.

J Earhart learned how to fly after the 1928 flight.

5 Write a statement of opinion based on the last sentence of the selection.

_____

_____

_____

_____

_____

Name _____

Read the selection. Then answer the questions that follow.

About *Shrek*

The animated film *Shrek* tells the story of a big green ogre named Shrek, who lives contentedly alone in a forest in an imaginary land called Duloc. Although big and fearsome, Shrek is really a kindhearted being who enjoys his solitary life. However, Shrek's peaceful life in the woods is disrupted when Lord Farquaad, the ruler of Duloc, decides to banish all the fairy-tales from the land, and Shrek's home becomes overrun by the displaced fairy-tale creatures.

When Shrek's home is invaded, he sets out to find Lord Farquaad and to persuade the ruler to take the fairy-tale creatures back, so that they can go home and Shrek can live again in peace. Lord Farquaad tells Shrek that he'll take the fairy-tale beings back on the condition that Shrek finds the princess Fiona, so that Farquaad can marry her. Shrek begins his journey to find Fiona and is accompanied by his loyal and talkative friend the donkey. The adventures that follow make for a very entertaining film, with a surprising ending.

The 2001 film is based on the children's book *Shrek!* by the award-winning cartoonist and author William Steig. During his early life, Steig made his living as an acclaimed cartoonist, creating thousands of drawings for the magazine *The New Yorker*. At the age of sixty-one, Steig began writing and illustrating children's books, and he soon earned awards for his books, including the Caldecott Medal for his third children's book *Sylvester and the Magic Pebble*.

Steig continued to create new books throughout his long life, writing *Shrek!* when he was in his nineties. Like other works by Steig, this tale about the goodhearted green ogre emphasizes the values of independence, resourcefulness, and tolerance of others. The movie and the book are well worth seeing and reading.

Turn the page.

Answer the questions below.

1 **Which of the following is a statement of fact based on the first paragraph?**

   A The film *Shrek* was set in the imaginary land of Duloc.

   B Shrek was the most fearsome monster in Duloc.

   C Lord Farquaad hated all fairy-tales.

   D Shrek's kind heart was evident to all who met him.

2 **Which of the following sentences contains a statement of opinion?**

   F Shrek's friend, the donkey, was rarely quiet.

   G Steig began writing children's books late in life.

   H *Shrek* the movie is based on a book by the same title.

   J *Sylvester and the Magic Pebble* deserved a medal.

3 **If you wanted to verify the statements of fact about Steig's life, which of the following reference sources would you use?**

   A a dictionary

   B a map of Duloc

   C a biography about Steig

   D a social studies textbook

4 **Based on information about Steig's books, what is Sylvester probably like?**

_____

_____

_____

_____

5 **List a statement of opinion from the last paragraph of the selection.**

_____

_____

_____

_____

Name _____

Read the selection. Then answer the questions that follow.

Cordelia's Discovery

Cordelia's mother had asked her to clean up her very messy room. Cordelia didn't mind cleaning; she just preferred to do other things, like read poems or collect rocks. However, she knew her mother was right about her room being a mess, so she made a plan to get it in order.

First, she picked up all the clothes that were lying about the room and put them in the laundry basket. Next, she took all the books and put them back on the shelves. Finally, she decided to put away the toys that were scattered about, and as she was reaching for a rubber lizard, she noticed something shiny next to it.

"My mica!" she said. It was a rock she thought she had lost. Cordelia's prize possession was her rock collection, and the mica had been missing a long time. Looking around her cleared room, Cordelia saw the perfect place for her rock collection, a small table, and began arranging all the rocks on it.

Turn the page.

Answer the questions below.

1 Which of the following events occured last?

A Cordelia's mother asked her to clean her room.

B Cordelia put away all the toys in her room.

C Cordelia put her books back on the shelves.

D Cordelia picked up her clothes and put them in a basket.

2 What clue word helps you know the second thing in Cordelia's plan to clean up her room?

F then

G finally

H however

J next

3 Which of the following events occurred before Cordelia found her piece of mica?

A She arranged her rock collection on a small table.

B She showed her mother her recently cleaned room.

C She reached for a rubber lizard.

D She saw the perfect place to put her rocks.

4 Why is Cordelia so happy to find the piece of mica?

_____

_____

_____

_____

_____

_____

Name _____

Read the selection. Then answer the questions that follow.

Vladimir the Goldfish

There once was a guy named Chris who had a beloved pet goldfish named Vladimir. Chris had gotten Vladimir at the local pet store, when Vlad, as Chris called him, was just a tiny fish, and now Vlad was growing rapidly. Chris was a conscientious pet owner, and he would thoroughly clean Vladimir's tank every day using a special vacuum and feed Vlad twice a day.

Vladimir loved to eat, and his favorite food was lettuce, although he would also consume the fish food Chris sprinkled in the water. Although Chris stuck to a regular feeding schedule, giving Vlad only the suggested amount of food, Vlad seemed to get bigger and bigger and bigger. After a few weeks, Chris noticed that Vlad was almost as big as the two-foot by two-foot tank, so Chris went out and bought a larger tank for Vlad to live in.

Although the new tank was five feet long and three feet wide, Vlad soon expanded in this new home as well, growing to be about four feet long in no time. At this point, Chris became quite worried, since he realized he would have to build another tank to accommodate Vlad, who was still eating just lettuce and a few sprinkles of fish food a day.

Chris and his friend Amy built a special tank for Vlad, and the tank was about half the size of Chris's apartment. Amy set up the seaweed plants and rocks in the tank by climbing into it using a ladder, and after she was done, she and Chris filled the tank with fresh water. Then they transferred Vlad to his new home, where Vlad splashed happily about making puddles on the apartment floor. Luckily, however, for Chris, Vlad stopped growing once he was in the new tank, and Chris was able to concentrate on other matters.

Turn the page.

Answer the questions below.

1 **Which of the following occurred first in the story?**

A Chris realized he would have to buy a new tank.

B Amy climbed into the tank to arrange the seaweed and rocks.

C Chris visited the local pet store.

D Vladimir splashed some puddles on the floor.

2 **Which of the following occurred right before Chris decided to build a new tank?**

F Chris asked Amy to help him with a project.

G Vladimir grew to be about four feet long.

H Amy and Chris filled a tank with fresh water.

J Vladimir stopped getting bigger.

3 **When did Vlad move into the tank Chris and Amy built?**

A right after Amy and Chris poured water into the tank

B right after Amy placed the seaweed plants and rocks in the tank

C right after Vlad stopped growing

D right after Vlad ate lettuce and sprinkles of fish food

4 **Which of the following words best describes Amy?**

F tired

G helpful

H talkative

J serious

5 **Name two events that occurred after Chris and Amy transfer Vlad to his third tank.**

_____

_____

_____

_____

_____

_____

_____

Name _____

Read the selection. Then answer the questions that follow.

Atalanta's Big Race

In Greek mythology, there are many stories about the heroine Atalanta, who was said to have sailed with the Argonauts and to have participated in the hunt of a great Calydonian boar. However, the most famous story about Atalanta has to do with romance and a running race.

Raised by bears and hunters, Atalanta became extremely swift and adept at hunting and other skills usually ascribed to boys. She could, in fact, outrun and outwrestle the boys in her land, and because she was not interested in getting married, Atalanta challenged her many suitors to running races. Knowing she could beat any man, she declared that she would marry anyone who could beat her in a foot race. Although many suitors tried to win her hand this way, Atalanta ran faster than all of them, until a man named Hippomenes came along.

Knowing he could not outrun Atalanta, Hippomenes sought the help of the goddess of love, Aphrodite. Aphrodite agreed to help the young man, giving him three beautiful golden apples to use during the race. When the day of the contest arrived, Hippomenes was ready, and when, as expected, Atalanta surged ahead of him, he threw the first golden apple in her path.

Distracted by its beauty, Atalanta paused to pick up the apple, and Hippomenes ran ahead of her. However, Atalanta soon caught up with him, so Hippomenes threw the second golden apple a little to the side. As she ran off the path, Hippomenes passed her a second time.

As they neared the finish line, Atalanta caught up and surpassed Hippomenes and was about to win the race, when the young suitor threw the final golden apple across her path and into the grass. She could not resist its loveliness, so while she was chasing the apple, Hippomenes won the race and her hand in marriage. Although Atalanta's carefree days were over, the couple was said to have been quite happy, often running together in the forest.

Turn the page.

Answer the questions below.

1 Which of the following occurred first in the story?

A Atalanta paused to pick up an apple from her path.

B Atalanta ran off the path to chase a golden apple.

C Hippomenes threw a golden apple into the grass.

D Hippomenes went to the goddess Aphrodite for help.

2 Which of the following occurred at the same time Atalanta was chasing the third golden apple?

F Hippomenes passed Atalanta a second time.

G Atalanta decided to take another path to the finish line.

H Hippomenes won the race and the right to marry Atalanta.

J Aphrodite gave Hippomenes another apple.

3 Which of the following occurred after Hippomenes threw the first golden apple?

A Atalanta picked it up.

B Atalanta ate the golden apple.

C Atalanta won the race and the right to marry Hippomenes.

D Atalanta stepped on the golden apple.

4 Why did Aphrodite give Hippomenes the golden apples?

_____

_____

_____

_____

_____

5 What event occurred after Hippomenes won the race?

_____

_____

_____